ADVICE TO
HOUSEHOLDERS

YOGA RESEARCH FOUNDATION
(Non-profit Organization)

AIMS AND OBJECTS

1. To spread the laws of spiritual life.

2. To promote understanding of the unity of life among all people, regardless of race, sect, creed and sex, and also to promote harmony among all religions by emphasizing the fundamental unity of all prophets, saints, sages and teachers.

3. To help suffering humanity by teaching the higher moral standards, prayers and meditation.

4. To give regular classes in the teachings of Yoga, Vedanta and Indian Philosophy.

5. To promote Universal Peace and Universal Love.

6. To promote the cultural growth of humanity on the basis of everlasting spiritual values of life.

7. To guide students and devotees all over the world.

8. To print and publish spiritual literature.

9. Anyone devoted to the ideals of truth, non-violence and purity can be a member of this Foundation.

Yoga Research Foundation
6111 S.W. 74th Avenue
South Miami, Florida 33143
Tel: (305) 666-2006

ISBN 0-934664-54-4

Library of Congress Catalog Card Number 89-051442

PRINTED IN THE UNITED STATES OF AMERICA

ADVICE TO HOUSEHOLDERS

by
Swami Jyotirmayananda

**Dedicated to
the householders of today
who are intent upon finding
the secrets of a successful marriage,
and are striving to establish a happy home.
In this congenial atmosphere their children
would grow to be the ideal men
and women of tomorrow,
paving the way for
peace and harmony
in the world.**

PUBLISHER'S NOTE

"Householders are the backbone of human society"—says Swami Jyotirmayananda in this inspiring book, *Advice to Householders*. All cultural advancement, all forms of progress that humanity is proud of are rooted in a healthy family life.

In our times technological advancement has made amazing strides. The space that physically separates one person from another is shrinking. Spaceships are even being sent out to explore the distant recesses of the universe and bring them within our reach. And yet, despite this conquest of physical space, human beings are unable to come close to each other in spiritual and psychological communion. There is so much disharmony and dissension in most families. There is insecurity in marital life. Even after living together for many years, a husband may divorce his wife, or a wife her husband. And the children must bear the brunt of growing up in a family with disharmony and dissension.

This present book contains a series of lectures given by Swami Jyotirmayananda to the Hindu community of Orlando, Florida, on October 29 and 30, 1988. Within these two days, in four sessions, Swami Jyotirmayananda covered a great range of topics related to householders. The audience listened to him with rapt attention, and many expressed the view that if a book were to be brought out containing these talks, it would be a great blessing for all those who seek harmony and peace in family life. This book is the result of their wishes.

This book gives a profound insight as well as practical guidance for unity between husband and wife, between parents and children, between family and society. The Hindu view of marriage brings a new vision in the meaning of human relationships. Swami Jyotirmayananda says: "Sense-pleasure (Bhoga) is not the goal of life. When sense-pleasure is given its proper place, then, it becomes a means to discovering spiritual union between two persons—husband and wife. When pleasure is not held as the highest in life then it becomes easy for a person to practise deeper adjustments for a harmonized family life. Yoga (union with God) is the goal of life."

What is true love? How should a child be educated? How should adverse situations be faced? How should Yoga be practised in daily life? How can one live a life of harmony and peace? What are the duties of a householder? How do we promote peace and harmony in the world? For the answers to these and many other vital questions turn to the pages of this book. You will find a wealth of insight that will bring a profound change in your life, and you will enjoy a new type of happiness beyond your imagination.

Undoubtedly this book will prove to be a fountain source of inspiration for married couples and householders all over the world who are seeking success in their married life.

We thank our staff for their devoted work leading to the printing and publication of this unique book.

May you attain success, harmony, peace, prosperity and Divine Enlightenment!

Swami Lalitananda
October 1989

**This book has been printed
to honor the following great souls,
whose sons (who wish to be anonymous)
have contributed towards the printing of
this book for the service of humanity:**

Behcharbhai Jivanbhai Patel (father)—Arakpardiwala
Daviben Bechcharbhai Patel (mother)

Lalbhai Khushalbhai Patel (father)—Munsadwala
Sitaben Lalbhai Patel (mother)

Chhitubhai Kanjibhai Patel (father)—Kachhiawadiwala
Bhuliben Chhitubhai Patel (late mother)

Kanaiyalal Chhotalal Vin (late father)—Bharuchwala
Mudrikaben Kanaiyalal Vin (mother)

Bhikhabhai Purshottamdass Patel (father)—Bandhaniwala
Chancelben Bhikhabhai Patel (mother)

**May God bless the donors
and their above-mentioned parents
with His choicest blessings!**

CONTENTS

1
FOR THE NEWLYWEDS

2
SAMSKARAS OR SACRAMENTS

3
AUSTERITY AND YAJNAS

4
EDUCATION

5
WHAT IS LOVE?

6
YOGA IN LIFE

7
UPASANA OR MEDITATION

Author Swami Jyotirmayananda

1

FOR THE NEWLYWEDS

*In every
human embodiment
and through all your relationships,
your goal is to accomplish spiritual evolution.
That goal is vital to your life, and it
must be the guiding light of your marriage.
Husband and wife must work together
in such a way that
both develop a relaxed mind,
a pure heart, a discerning intellect,
and a highly integrated
personality.*

MESSAGE TO NEWLYWEDS

Blessed Self-in-all, adorations!

Having grown in discipline and wisdom during your student days in *Brahmacharya Ashrama*—the first of the four stages of life outlined by Hindu tradition—you have now entered into the sacrament of marriage. You have become a *grihasthi* or a householder. In Sanskrit marriage is called *Vivaha Samskara*. *Vivaha* comes from the root *"vah" (vahan)* which means "to hold a responsibility, to carry through the stream of life." If you develop deep insight into this special responsibility, your life will become supremely fulfilling and joyous.

Karma Has Joined You Together

Out of countless souls, how do two people come together in a marriage relationship that is going to be intense and prolonged, making the greatest impact on their lives of all relationships that they can enter into? It is due to the law of *karma*. In the *karmic* process those souls need to assist each other in their spiritual evolution. In the highest sense, they enter into that most profound relationship of marriage to lead each other to Self-realization.

Helping Each Other Evolve

Alone, a person is unable to fulfill the various needs of the soul. Alone you cannot work out the fulfillment of your desires, and the sublimation of those ideas and fancies that remain unfulfilled. Alone you cannot work out your spiritual evolution. Therefore, in the Divine Plan, Nature brings people together to assist each other.

Through all the countless relationships you have had in countless embodiments, you have been evolving. From the point of the soul you are eternal. Remember the teachings of Lord Krishna:

> *Vaasaamsi jeernaani yathaa vihaaya*
> *Navaani grihnaati naro'paraani;*
> *Tathaa sareeraani vihaaya*
> *Jeernaani-Yanyaani samyaati navaani dehi.*

Just as a person gives up his old clothes to put on new ones, so the embodied soul, having discarded the worn out bodies, puts on new ones. (Gita 2/22)

In every human embodiment and through all your relationships, your goal is to accomplish spiritual evolution. That goal is vital to your life, and it must be the guiding light of your marriage. Husband and wife must work together in such a way that both develop a relaxed mind, a pure heart, a discerning intellect, and a highly integrated personality.

Most young people begin their amorous relationship with fervent expressions of their sweet sentiments and glorious hopes for their future. But gradually they allow their relationship to deteriorate into a purposeless interdependence in which the goal of life has been forgotten. You should not follow this course. If you do so, your marriage is a failure.

Husband and wife must do all that they can to encourage a Godward movement in one another. The husband should never become a tyrant who prohibits his wife from performing a prayer service *(puja)* because he does not feel like doing so at the moment. Similarly, a wife should not become upset and demanding if her husband wants to go to an *ashram* for *satsanga* (holy association) and she is unable to join him. Husband and wife should never "pull each other's legs" to keep the other from ascending higher on the spiritual ladder! If that type of attitude develops, their marriage will not be fulfilling.

It is only on the basis of Godward movement that you can build an enduring relationship. If you take God away from your life, your relationship will become shallow. Ideally both husband and wife should join hands in attending *satsanga* (good association), practising meditation, performing religious worship, prayer and other forms of *sadhana* (spiritual disciplines). Never feel that spiritual practices will upset your relationship; rather, they will promote a relationship that is profound and enduring.

If you are making the time for a little meditation, a little prayer, and a little *japa* (repetition of *mantra* or a Divine name) each day, if you celebrate sacred days and fast when possible, if you study the holy scriptures—such as the *Ramayana*, the *Gita*, or any scripture according to your faith—you will bring a special spiritual charm into your married life.

You should not develop the idea, "We are modern

now and therefore we should not go along with the old spiritual traditions." It is from your faith in religion and faith in God that you will receive special strength during severe problems of life. During situations that baffle all your intelligence, it is your faith that will come forward to help you.

Therefore, husband and wife should encourage each other towards spiritual development, towards being more faithful, more devoted, more religious, and more disciplined. When you help each other to be undisciplined and disorganized, you become enemies for each other. An undisciplined life is the fertile soil for all miseries in life.

Yoga Not Bhoga

In the Western world, you are constantly exposed to a materialistic attitude towards life that considers the pleasures of the senses as the highest goal. The moment materialistic people find diminution of pleasure in a relationship, they are ready to divorce their husband or wife and get married again.

According to the Hindu Dharma, this is an unhealthy attitude. Sense-pleasure *(bhoga)* is not the goal of life. However, when sense-pleasure is given its proper place, it becomes a means to discovering spiritual union between husband and wife. When pleasure is not held as the highest attainment in life, it becomes easy for a person to make the deeper adjustments that are necessary for a harmonized family life. Yoga (union with God), not *bhoga*, is the goal of life.

Age with Dignity

Think of what often happens to people in a pleasure-oriented, materialistic society when they age: they have no control over their minds, they become intolerant and highly irritable. No matter what wonderful ideas they might have had when they were young, when they age those ideas vanish. They might have been bright and relaxed personalities once, but as time passes, they become mentally debilitated, weak-willed and ill-tempered.

The irritability of old people has become proverbial. It is said, "The wind howls, but it calms down in a while; but not so with ill-tempered people—they continue howling day and night." Do not let yourself age in this fashion.

If you are not careful, as you grow older the things that you once hated in others will become a part of your personality. However, if you are careful during the *Brahmacharya* and *Grihastha* stages of life, you will avoid this regrettable state. If you lead a life of discipline and devotion to *dharma* (righteousness), as you age you will enjoy increasing inner peace and spiritual contentment. You will become more relaxed, stronger in spirit, more accomplished in controlling the mind—a source of happiness to yourself and to the world around you.

Adapt and Adjust

In every marriage and in every family situation—no matter how perfectly matched two people may be, or how agreeable the various family members may be towards each other—there are many things to which you have to adapt and adjust. There are many unknown things that you will discover about each other, and you will face a constant challenge to understand one another and to maintain harmony in the relationship. It is by accepting the challenge and making yourself more disciplined that you begin to discover the deeper meaning behind relationships.

Throughout your life as a householder you are being disciplined by the Divine Plan. If you were told by a teacher, for example, to get up at 4:00 o'clock in the morning for meditation, prayer and other spiritual disciplines, you would say it is too much to do. But when your little baby cries in the night, you get up immediately and run around, doing whatever is necessary—without hesitation—to comfort the child.

So you see, nature has a special way of disciplining you in family life, of urging you to be self-sacrificing again and again. As you begin to learn the art of sacrificing your little Self, of stepping beyond the expectations of the ego, you are learning deeper lessons of life that will promote peace and harmony in the family. This will prepare you for serving society in an effective manner and will accelerate your own spiritual evolution.

Do Not Be Afraid To Be "Real"

Your striving sincerely to promote harmony and adjustment within a marriage does not mean that day-by-day there will be perfect smoothness—no raising of the voice, no misunderstanding, no quarrel. When householders brag before others, saying: "We have been married for thirty years, and we have never had a single quarrel," then within the very next year you may hear that they are divorcing each other.

The fact is that it is unnatural to live with people and not face situations of misunderstanding. There will always be a little raising of voices, a little expression of displeasure, a little quarrelling. If two persons in a marriage relationship never argue, nor show any displeasure, there are two possibilities to explain it: there is fear and artificiality in the relationship, or it is the marriage of two enlightened sages.

In real love between two people, there must be flexibility. Each one must be able to say what is on his or her mind, and the other person must be able to listen. Neither must be afraid to express themselves thinking, "If I say what is on my mind, there will be trouble. Therefore, let me continue smiling."

If fear controls the relationship, it is not a real marriage. Therefore both partners must learn to adapt and adjust. That is the great art in life. Where there is self-sacrifice, patience and endurance, a deeper love develops—a love of a higher type that is sweet and sublime. But where there is no genuine adjustment between partners, where there is only yielding to each other with bitterness, marriage becomes a great pressure to the soul that is carried on day by day. Under this situation of stress, life becomes very shallow and even the slightest difficulty or misunderstanding can cause the husband or wife to file for a divorce.

Adore God in Each Other

In an ideal Hindu marriage, the husband worships the *Devi* (Goddess) in the wife and the wife worships God (in the form of Krishna, Vishnu, or Rama) in her husband. And when there is a child you worship God in the child. You should develop the attitude that God is the innermost reality within every person. To the extent that you understand this truth, each member of your family becomes an expression of God and you are worshipping, loving and serving God through everyone you are related to. This attitude elevates human relationships and helps you to develop an amazing degree of endurance in even the worst of situations.

No one should expect perfection in a marriage relationship without intense self-effort. Whatever degree of perfection is attained has to evolve by mutual love, by austerity, by adapting and adjusting, and by turning to God for strength.

Further again, the goal is not perfection in the relationship itself—the goal is movement towards God. By the time death terminates your union, both of you should be ready to attain Self-realization. This is your goal. If that goal is kept in view, everything in your life becomes meaningful and significant. Without that spiritual objective, you face a world of unimaginable stress, sorrow and grief.

Derive Strength From God

Allow your minds to flow Godwards: learn to serve God, adore God and love God in each other. When problems baffle your mind, seek guidance from God within you through prayer, *japa*, and surrender. At the same time, don't wait for a difficult situation to develop to turn to God. There is a saying of Saint Kabira, *"Dukh me sumiran sab kare, sukh me kare na koy. Jo sukh me sumiran kare to dukh kahe ko hoy."* The meaning is, "Everyone, when put under stress, turns to God; but the moment that stressing situation fades, he forgets about God. If he were to turn to God even in pleasant conditions, then why should there be adversity for him?"

There is a parable about a man who went out to pick coconuts. He climbed to the top of a tall tree laden with coconuts and suddenly he looked down and felt dizzy. He prayed, "Oh God, I know I can't get down from this height without falling and killing myself. If only You would spare me this time, I will give all these coconuts to a temple as an offering." Thus saying, he slowly started coming down, emboldened by the courage he had gained through prayer. But when he came down a little bit further, he thought to himself, "I will give away only 75% of the coconuts. Why to give 100%?" When he had come down halfway, he began thinking, "Well, God doesn't need all that anyway. I'll give 50%." When he came down completely and his feet touched the ground, he had forgotten all about God.

So, as you face the challenges of life, do not be like the man in the parable. Do not wait for adversity to turn to God for strength, forgetting Divine grace when the adversity passes away. Rather, day by day, learn to enjoy the sweetness of devotion and surrender to God. At every moment, feel that God sustains you and enjoy the sweetness of that Divine sustenance.

Be Inspired by Spiritual Ideals

According to Hindu Dharma, marriage is a sacrament, and the ideal of enduring and sacrificing love is presented in Hindu literature in the union of Rama and Sita, Savitri and Satyavan, and Nala and Damayanti.

Study the *Ramayana* for the story of Rama and Sita, and the *Mahabharata* for the story of Savitri and Satyavan, Nala and Damayanti.

These couples were ideals, embodiments of perfection—but you should try to emulate their example as much as possible. In the type of self-effacing love that they epitomize, all the deepest values of life flourish. But in love that is only pleasure-seeking, good qualities of the soul are thwarted and stunted.

Bring Forth Children for Greatness

One of your greatest responsibilities in marriage is having children and preparing those children for the spiritual and material challenges of life. As your children carry on the name of your family, they must also make a meaningful contribution to humanity—to the world family. They may become successful personalities in science, in the arts, in philosophy, in religion, or in any of the various branches of learning. By their wisdom and understanding, they may sow seeds of harmony and peace and spiritual understanding among others.

Be an Inspiration to Your Children

Children must be taught by your example. If you yourself do not do what you teach your children to do, then you will not succeed as parents. If you ask your children to get up early in the morning, then you must pursue the same right course of action and start doing so yourself. If you ask your children to be patient and thoughtful and unselfish, you must manifest the same Divine qualities in your own personalities.

Plant Good Impressions Right from the Start

There is a *Puranic* story about Madalasa, a queen who was enlightened. Whenever she became pregnant, she kept her mind engaged in meditating and worshipping God. When the child was born, she cradled it gently, singing the following song: *"Shuddhosi Buddhosi Niranjanosi, Samsara maya parivarjitosi."* This inspiring song means: "O child, you are not the body, you are the spirit; you are enlightened, you are pure *Atman*—the Self. You are free of the taints of the world-process." As each of her children grew up, they became highly philosophical individuals and eventually enlightened saints.

All your thoughts, feelings and actions influence the unconscious mind of your child. Whatever you present before your children, even when they are infants, makes its impression. In fact the child begins to learn even before it is born. All the thoughts that enter the mind of the mother while the child is still growing within her impinge upon the mind of the child. So Hindu scriptures have given great insight into this prenatal stage of education.

Thus it is a great responsibility for a married couple to bring forth souls, to provide what is needed for their physical and mental well-being, to prepare them for society, and to encourage their spiritual evolution. These are duties that every *grihasthi* (householder) must take very seriously.

When you understand that nature has given you this tremendous project, and you pursue the project diligently, the rewards are great and the joys are intense. As you strive to promote a harmonized family life, you enjoy deeper love in human relations and deeper warmth and sweetness of life. Even in old age you will feel relaxed, peaceful and fulfilled. If, like Queen Madalasa, you both become enlightened sages and succeed in guiding your children to enlightenment as well, you have fulfilled the responsibilities of household life to the utmost, and attained all there is to attain as well!

May God bless you!

THE FOUR PURPOSES OF LIFE

The *Vedas* have outlined four purposes of life, which are known as *purusharthas*. The first of these is *dharma*, or righteousness, which refers to the ethical value of life. To have meaning, life must be rooted in *dharma*.

The next purpose of life is *artha*, the material value of life. *Artha* refers to your efforts to acquire property and possessions—to make yourself secure in the material world.

The third is known as *kama*—the vital value of life—which refers to establishing joyous relationships with family members and friends, and with other people around you in society. If that healthy relationship is not there, all one's prosperity is worth nothing.

The next and the ultimate purpose of life is *moksha* or liberation. This is the spiritual value of life in its infinite measure.

In an ideal and balanced plan, a person must be rooted in *dharma*—the ethical value of life. Without transgressing ethical values, one should establish meaningful social relationships *(kama)* and secure material means *(artha)*. One should then utilize his social and material wealth for intensifying his *dharma* and for moving towards *moksha* or liberation.

However, in a disbalanced and aberrant society, this ideal plan is ignored. *Kama* and *artha* are considered ends in themselves, and are not regulated by *dharma* as they should be. If unregulated *artha* and *kama* become the central focus of your life, you will be led to increasing stress, grief and frustration.

If you earn money without having your roots in *dharma*, that money will not give you peace. You cannot buy any happiness through unethical means—no matter how much money you obtain. The richest millionaires are often the most unhappy people. You may own a plane that can fly you to Switzerland for breakfast, to New York for lunch, and to London for dinner, but all this does not give you true happiness.

Many people have the idea that if they became millionaires overnight, by winning a lottery or by another similar piece of good fortune, things will become wonderful. They think that the solution to all their problems rests upon money. But that is a serious mistake. If someone were to become a millionaire overnight, many things would certainly change—but not necessarily for the better.

A rich person never knows whether he is receiving love and affection for their own sake or because of their money. In most cases, life becomes cheap, without any spiritual value. As greed is enhanced, one continues to hanker for more and more, yet is never fulfilled.

The Story of King Yayati

The scriptures tell the story of King Yayati, an ancient king, who, like others of his day, had lived a long, long time. One day Yayati noticed old age coming, and although he had enjoyed the pleasures of life intensely during his life, he suddenly became worried that now he would be devoid of pleasures. He saw a dark future brooding over him.

Since it was possible in those days for one person to transfer his youth to another, King Yayati asked his young children if any one of them would take his age in exchange for their youth. One of his children, who possessed great dispassion towards the pleasures of life even at a tender age, replied, "O father, I will be glad to exchange my youth for your age." And so the exchange was made and Yayati became young again, and again he lived a life of intense pleasure.

But again, time passed on as it must. Time never stands still. Even if someone were to give you a thousand years, those years would pass away some day. Millions of years, millions of Earth planets, millions of solar systems come and go—so what to speak of the short time-fragment of one lifetime?

And as time passed, King Yayati again found his body aging. However, his craving for pleasure was still as strong as ever! Thus he realized the impossibility of ever satisfying one's worldly desires by merely having more and more experiences. Only through increasing discrimination and dispassion can one experience fulfillment and peace.

Desires will never end. Bhartrihari says, *"Trishnaa na jeernaa, vayameva jeerna,"* which means, "Craving does not age, it does not decay, but we ourselves continue to age." In fact, as a human being ages, his craving seems to become more and more youthful.

Moksha—The Central Goal

Life is like a house. Without *dharma*, this house is without a foundation. Without *artha*, this house has no walls. Without *kama*, it has no furnishings, and without *moksha*, it has no roof.

Therefore, in a harmonious spiritual plan of life, *dharma* is the basis, and it should not be overstepped. Keeping *dharma* as the root, you earn money, utilize your wealth in a proper way and, in that process, you acquire friends and relatives who provide a joyous family and social life.

But, the joys of *artha* and *kama* are only a means to an end. That end is *moksha*, or liberation. If *moksha* is not kept before your mind as the goal, then life becomes like a ship without a destination. But, if you keep *moksha* in view, life becomes a process of discovering the boundless power, glory and beauty of the Self.

THE FOUR STAGES OF LIFE

According to the ancient Hindu culture, life is divided into four stages called *Ashramas*. These four stages are: *Brahmacharya* (student), *Grihastha* (householder), *Vanaprastha* (forest-dweller) and *Sanyasa* (renunciate).

The Ancient Plan

Considering the duration of human life to be one hundred years, the sages of ancient India taught that the first twenty-five years are to be devoted to *Brahmacharya* or student life. The second twenty-five years (up to fifty years of age) should be spent in *Grihastha* or householder life. Then, having renounced family life and adopted *Vanaprastha*, one should live a life of austerity and study of scriptures up to the age of seventy-five. The last twenty-five years are to be devoted to the attainment of liberation by adopting the order of *Sanyasa* or renunciation.

This is an ideal plan of life that was suited to the needs and circumstances of life in those times. Of course it cannot suit all people of all ages. In the modern world, in which people generally do not live for such a long time, the time allotted for the different *Ashramas* must be adjusted to suit the present situation.

BRAHMACHARYA—
THE STUDENT STAGE

Brahmacharya is the first stage of life. In this student stage one learns to live a life of austerity and discipline which lays down the foundation for future success in life.

In a restricted sense, *brahmacharya* implies abstaining from sex pleasures. In a wider sense, *brahmacharya* is a plan of total disciplining of the body, mind and senses for receiving education, and for moving towards the final goal—*Brahman* or God-realization.

Sex-Abstinence

In the *Brahmacharya* stage of life, young people are asked to avoid sexual intimacy and keep their minds away from the things that awaken sexual passion in the mind. Students are led to understand that there is a profound responsibility involved in handling one's sex life—and that if that responsibility is not properly understood one's whole life can be wasted.

The Importance of Discipline

If one is not disciplined at an early age, one later falls a prey to numerous evils such as bad association, drugs, drinking, and manifold perversions of the modern materialistic society. Life then becomes a curse.

If one is left "free" to do whatever comes to mind, according to whim, he becomes a lunatic. One who is truly free possesses a clear mind and the ability to control his senses. Freedom comes where there is order and discipline, not where there is slavery to the senses.

When you were small, you might have hated your parents when they were disciplining you; but upon growing up you were grateful to them because they did so. As you matured you understood that it was their responsibility to handle you well, to train you well. You came into their lives as a tender stranger, and it was the duty of your parents to give you a sense of values, to educate you, to prepare you for bigger responsibilities in society and for higher purposes in life.

Discipline then, is most important, but there is no one easy answer about how and when discipline should be practised. Thus, parents must reflect deeply in order to learn this important art. As a general guideline, firmness must be blended with sweetness. You should be stern and firm when necessary, as well as loving, tender and sweet. From deep within, you should be always guided by love. True love, whether it is between mature people, parents, or children, need never be afraid of disciplining.

GRIHASTHA ASHRAMA—
THE HOUSEHOLDER STAGE

Householders have a great responsibility. They are the backbone of society. The whole social structure depends upon householders. Householders bring forth children, and those new generations must bring new greatness to society in the fields of spirituality, science, arts, literature, and in all forms of higher culture.

The Responsibility and Joys of Having Good Children

According to the Hindu Dharma, householders may plan to bring forth a child with special qualities and talents. They practise austerity and devout meditation to achieve this objective.

According to the philosophy of the *Vedas*, a child is an evolving soul. It is not born in a family just as an accident. It is drawn to a family where it can find the best situation for its evolution. If a married couple were to live a life of austerity and devotion, they would draw a righteous or an evolved soul as their son or daughter. By adopting special attitudes and meditations, they may plan to have a child with special qualities such as patriotism, heroism, scientific talents, artistic skill, and so forth.

If you read the scriptures you will find that even the Divine Incarnation, Krishna, practised intense austerities for twelve years to beget a child. Even Krishna the Divine did so—why? To set an example for others—to teach the lesson that the goal in human life is not sheer pleasure, but there is a deeper purpose. You do not bring a child into the world just as a by-product of pleasure but you regulate your pleasure so that you may bring a child with special virtues.

Bringing into your family a greater soul, and then educating that soul and allowing the soul to evolve in a congenial environment gives you an opportunity for a greater form of good *karma*. The positive interrelation of the soul of the child with the souls of the parents is an important aspect of *karmic* fulfillment. As you help your child create positive *karmas* for himself, you are creating better *karmas* for yourself and for society. The child, unconsciously, is always influencing you.

In a humorous story it is told how King Akbar was once playing with his little grandson while court was in session. Suddenly the little boy climbed upon Akbar's shoulder and grabbed his moustache. That was the greatest crime that one could commit when the court was in session.

So, King Akbar looked at Birbal and said, "What punishment should we give to this young criminal who snatches at my moustache?" Birbal replied, "Your Majesty, he has every right to do so, because he is the emperor of emperors." King Akbar said, "How so? Prove it; otherwise I will have to deal with you sternly." Birbal said, "Please, your majesty, give me some time and then you will understand."

Then one day Birbal brought a snake (which he alone knew was non-poisonous) into the court and let it loose while the little boy was right there. The boy rushed to catch the snake, laughing, and Akbar turned back in fear. At this, Birbal said, "Here is your proof. He who is the emperor of emperors—he has no fear."

As the story suggests, parents have a lot to learn from their children. Caring for the spirit that has come to you as a child in a little body helps you discipline and shape the inner structure of your own life as well, and at the same time, helps you enjoy a sweetness and tenderness

which otherwise you might not have expressed through
your personality. You may be terribly worried about
something, yet your child is always relaxed. The moment
you approach your child you begin to smile!

VANAPRASTHA ASHRAMA—
STAGE OF AUSTERITY AND REFLECTION

Ideally a married couple should expect to have one
or two children, and then they should adopt complete
brahmacharya (continence). For the majority of people,
the absence of sexual relationship may seem an end of
their marital joy. But it is not so. Rather, when a relationship is based upon pleasure, it is shallow, insecure, and
fleeting. As a deeper union is established between husband and wife, there opens up a new dimension of joy as
they assist each other in their spiritual growth.

As time passes by, one should be prepared to transcend one's family, and become wholly devoted to the
good of humanity. With this idea in view, in old times,
people renounced their families and went to a forest to
practise austerity, to study scriptures, and in turn to
impart knowledge to others. Many devoted their lives to
teaching children who were sent to forest-schools for
receiving education.

In modern times, the same ideal may be practised,
though you do not have to go to forests. You may prepare
yourself in such a way that, after retiring from your job,
you are able to share your knowledge and experience
with the young, growing children of your locality or community. Instead of being confined to homes for the

elderly, you should continue to interact with the younger generation, thus making your life as well as theirs richer and more meaningful.

If such a modern approach to *Vanaprastha* were adopted, the minds of the elderly would continue to remain bright, and an elderly person would continue to be a joy to himself and to society. Instead of being scorned and ridiculed, the elderly would be received with great honor and love.

SANYASA ASHRAMA— THE STAGE OF RENUNCIATION

With the passage of time, you may develop intense *vairagya* or dispassion towards the transient pleasures of the senses. Then, you may seek to be formally initiated into *Sanyasa* or the order of renunciation at an *ashram*, or you may become mentally a *sanyasi* and continue to perform your duties towards the good of all. Both ideals have been adopted in India. The actual goal is mental *sanyasa*: a mind that comprehends that "I am one with God. Nothing belongs to me. All this is *Brahman*."

The project before a *sanyasi* is to attain *mukti* or liberation—to become united with God. This ideal is to be achieved even in one's lifetime. It is the most exalted attainment—the goal that the soul has been striving to attain through countless embodiments.

As a *sanyasi* ascends the ladder of spiritual evolution, he becomes a source of inspiration for others. According to the *Gita*, such a *sanyasi* is ever devoted to the good of others: *"Sarva bhoota hite rataah."*

Variations on the Theme

These four stages may not be adopted by every individual. An individual who has attained extraordinary *vairagya* or dispassion during *Brahmacharya Ashrama* may choose in a healthy and mature way not to enter *Grihastha Ashrama*. He remains a *brahmachari* (a celibate) throughout his life. Such a person is called a *Naishthika Brahmachari*—one who has taken the vow of *brahmacharya* for his whole life.

If a *brahmachari* , due to very advanced impressions or *shubha samskaras*, is able to transmute his urge for pleasure into an urge for liberation and go directly into *sanyasa*, parents should not be upset nor view this as something tragic. It is due to very good *karma* from the past. However, parents should look deeply into their child's mind to determine if the child is choosing *sanyasa* because of some frustration or immaturity. If so, it would be wise for the parents to discourage his choice, because he will not succeed.

Adopting *sanyasa* should stem from full confidence within the student. If he does not have that powerful urge, then he will go astray in the name of *Brahmacharya*. The path of *sanyasa* requires a resolute march on a heroic path and it should not be adopted on the basis of simple sentiment. The strength to make this choice belongs to only a small number who have developed great aspiration for Self-realization.

It requires a tremendous power to step beyond the biological urge which has chased the soul from life to life. But with the power of *vairagya* a, person may step beyond it, and allow himself to be disciplined by a spiritual teacher until passion is completely transmuted into *ojas shakti* (spiritual energy)—and that is the goal. Whether you are a *brahmachari*, or a *grihasthi*, the goal is to acquire, even when you are alive, a mind that does not consider yourself as a physical body.

Bhishma in the *Mahabharata* is an example of a *Naishthika Brahmachari*. Because of his mastery over his senses, he had developed the psychic power of controlling his death at his will. Some great personalities such as Sri Shankaracharya embraced *sanyasa* without ever entering into householder life. These enlightened personalities have no need to follow the ancient plan of *Ashramas*. They are enlightened souls who began with *brahmacharya* and through *brahmacharya* attained *Brahman*—the goal of life.

Regardless of the exact path one chooses to follow, the movement towards liberation is not a selfish project. Rather, it is a sublime project wherein selfishness is sacrificed, the little self is negated, and one becomes a fountain source of all that is true, good and beautiful.

Bhagavan Krishna

2

SAMSKARAS
OR SACRAMENTS

"May my mind
be full of knowledge.
May I gain willpower.
May I perform my duties
with reflection and devotion.
May I possess an unwavering mind.
May I be endowed with discrimination
so that I may realize the Truth.
May my senses be healthy and strong.
May my life be permeated
with the spirit of sacrifice
and may it be filled with the
songs of Sama Veda."

THE EARLIEST SAMSKARAS AND PRENATAL EDUCATION

Samskaras literally mean impressions. But they also refer to special rituals or sacraments which create positive impressions *(shubha samskaras)* in the mind. The ancient sages evolved a highly advanced technique of spiritualizing the life of a person through the performance of *samskaras.* These *samskaras* are purificatory rites; they spiritualize the special events of one's life from the time of conception to the time of one's death and the cremation of the body.

In the life of a Hindu, there are fifty two *Samskaras,* of which ten are most important: *Garbhadhanam, Pumsavanam, Simantonnayanam, Jatakarma, Namakaranam, Annaprasanam, Chudakaranam, Upanayanam, Samavartanam and Vivah.* In addition some samskaras, such as worship of God, are performed daily, and some are performed on special occasions. *Shraddha,* the special spiritual rite for the peace and the upliftment of the souls of the forefathers, is performed on special days.

After completing *Grihastha Ashrama* (householder stage), one performs a special *samskara* for entering *Vanaprastha Ashrama* (stage of austerity and reflection). After this stage, ideally, one performs a special spiritual rite to enter *Sanyasa* (order of renunciation) and devotes the balance of his life to pursuing the path to enlighten-ment and sharing his knowledge with humanity.

Garbhadhanam

As it has been pointed out before, according to Hindu thought, parents have the choice to draw to themselves children of their choice from the souls in the subtle plane waiting to be reborn. If parents have disci-plined themselves with the idea of having a highly evolved soul in their family, they will be able to do so.

Keeping this in view, husband and wife perform special prayers and chant certain *mantras* before their sexual union. Amidst the vibrations of the Vedic *mantras* the child is conceived. If they strongly envision a saint in their family, the child will turn out to be a devotee of God. If they envision a genius in science or arts, the child will grow up with that inclination.

Pumsavanam

In the third month of pregnancy, it is believed that the physical and the vital sheaths of the child are formed. A special ritual is performed and *Vedic mantras* are chanted for the well-being of the growing fetus.

Simantonnayanam

In the seventh month of pregnancy, the mental and other higher sheaths of the child are in the making. At this time *mantras* are recited for the protection of the mother and the child.

Jata Karma

This *samskara* is performed immediately after the birth of the child. The father welcomes the newborn child with the chanting of *mantras*, and prays for the health, long life, intelligence and well-being of the child.

What Is The Real Identity of Your Child?

It is important to remember that the child is an embodied soul that has passed through many embodiments and belonged to many families in the past. Parents have drawn a spirit—a soul that has existed from beginningless time and will continue to do so for eternity. In fact, the soul in every individual is essentially the Divine Self.

The mutual *karmas* of parents and the incarnating soul bring about the birth of a child. In the scheme of *karmic* fructifications, father and mother both need to interact with a soul in the form of their child. The child in turn needs to receive bitter and sweet experiences as it grows under the care of the parents. From a broad point of view, the parents have to learn from their child as much as the child needs to learn from them.

Education Begins Even Prior to Birth

According to the Hindu thought education begins even while the embryo is growing within the womb of the mother. If the mother's mind is influenced by higher ideals during that time, it will create deep impressions in the brain cells of the child. The following stories from the scriptures will illustrate this point.

The Story of Abhimanyu

A story is told about how Abhimanyu, the son of Arjuna and Subhadra, acquired the technique of piercing Chakra-Vyuha—the most difficult of army formations. When Abhimanyu was still in the womb, his mother was listening intently to Arjuna's words about the techniques heroic warriors adopted to pierce special army formations. When Arjuna began to describe how the warrior should come out of the *Vyuha* (the army formation), Subhadra fell asleep.

Later, as a young warrior, Abhimanyu assisted his uncles in the famous war of the Mahabharata. On one occasion, he had to break the Chakra-Vyuha formation and he did so with skill, but he was not confident about how to come out of it. He fought heroically, paving the way for the victory of the Pandavas (his uncles), however, he could not come out alive; he was killed.

His death is attributed to the fact that his mother slept while the last stage of the technique was being described by his father while Abhimanyu was yet in the womb. This story shows the importance of the thoughts that are entertained by the mother during her pregnancy, and how they influence the mind of the child.

The Story of Prahlad

During Devasura Sangram (when Gods and demons fought), Hiranyakashipu, the Lord of demons, was away from his capital city and in his absence gods captured his wives and kept them in prison. One of those wives was pregnant with Prahlad at the time.

When Sage Narada visited that divine prison and extolled the glory of Lord Vishnu, Prahlad's mother listened to his inspiring words. As a result, when Prahlad was born, he showed devotional inclinations from the very start. It was, however, against the wishes of the demon King that his child should become a devotee of God, and he tried to destroy Prahlad by various methods. Prahlad survived all attempts upon his life because he was protected by Lord Vishnu. Eventually Lord Vishnu destroyed Hiranyakashipu, and Prahlad became one of the greatest devotees of God.

As these stories show, education begins very early through the influence of the mother. One's mother not only gives physical nutrition, but she also nourishes the subtle body of the child through her thoughts and her feelings. Naturally, if the mother has been well-disciplined prior to bearing a child, she will spontaneously implant the best of impressions within her children. If she has not, the impressions gathered by the child's mind will depend upon the varying moods of the mother's mind. Every mood, feeling, thought, and experience of joy and sorrow will continue to impinge upon the mind of the child.

SAMSKARAS OF CHILDHOOD AND ADOLESCENCE

After the birth of the child, the following *samskaras* are performed at different stages of the child's growth: *Namakaranam, Annaprasanam, Chudakaranam, Upanayanam* and *Samavartanam*.

The ritual of *samskara* has three purposes: 1. *Malapanayan* or removal of impurities. 2. *Atishayadhan* or enrichment. 3. *Nyunangpurak* or supplementation. For example, when a farmer brings wheat from the field, it must first be subjected to removal of the husk. Secondly, it is dried in the sun and then turned into flour, and the flour is then enriched by adding vitamins or other needed nutrients. Thirdly, after cooking bread, one must prepare vegetables or some soup as supplementary articles to be eaten along with bread.

By the performance of *samskaras* the same three processes are applied to human personality: the removal of defects, the cultivation of virtues and the attainment of educational skill, and the development of spiritual qualifications.

Namakaranam

On an auspicious day, the child is given a meaningful name with the recitation of *Vedic mantras*. This is done on the tenth, eleventh, twelfth, eighteenth, or nineteenth day. If for some reason the naming ceremony is delayed, it may be done on the hundredth day. In general people in India give Divine names to their children—Rama, Krishna, Saraswati, Lakshmi. An inspiring name is uplifting for the child and for all those who will come into contact with the child. Unknowingly you repeat a Divine *Mantra* by giving a Divine name to your child.

Annaprasanam

In the sixth month, the child is given solid food for the first time. At this time, *mantras* are recited and oblations are offered to Deities. When food, which is a manifestation of God, is sanctified by the chant of *mantras*, it nourishes the body and mind in a special way, and helps to embellish one's life with spiritual qualities.

Chudakaranam

This is the ceremony in which the head of the child is shaved. It is performed in the first or the third year. It may also be performed in the fifth, seventh, tenth or eleventh year. Certain impurity that might have lingered with the child from birth is now removed. In addition, shaving of the head is symbolic of renouncing all worldly desires. In a subtle way the child is reminded of the Divine project of attaining God-realization.

Upanayanam

The literal meaning of this term is "bringing near"— implying that the child is brought near a *guru* (a spiritual preceptor). He is invested with a sacred thread (*yajnopavita*) and initiated into the sacred *Gayatri Mantra*. With this initiation he attains his second birth—he is now born to unfold and discover his spiritual nature.

Significance of the Sacred Thread

The sacred thread consists of three threads knotted together. This means that whoever wears the sacred thread has adopted the path of disciplining the mind, speech and body by controlling thoughts, words and actions. The three threads also symbolize God, Who has three aspects: *Sat* (Existence), *Chit* (Knowledge) and *Ananda* (Bliss). The project in your life is to realize your essential Divine nature: *Sat-Chit-Ananda*.

On receiving this sacred thread, a boy enters *Brahmacharya Ashrama*—the student stage of life which is characterized by discipline and devotion to studies. According to tradition, a girl may not wear a sacred thread—but she is equally entitled to repeat the *Gayatri Mantra*, and discipline herself for receiving education, for enriching her life with spiritual qualities, and attaining the goal of life—Self-realization.

The sacred thread is a constant reminder of your spiritual ideal: You are not this physical body. You are essentially the Immortal Self. You have limitless possibilities. Amazing things can be accomplished by leading a life of discipline and austerity.

A *brahmachari* should read about the lives of great men—spiritual personalities such Swami Vivekananda, Mahatma Gandhi and other saints and sages—and be inspired by them.

In daily life, a student should practise Yoga exercises, *pranayams*, meditation and *japa* (repetition of *mantra*). This will keep him free of the stress and strain of the modern world, and enable him to cultivate Divine virtues such as humility, devotion to God, serenity of mind, fearlessness, etc. His life will become a great blessing for himself and for others.

Samavartanam

This marks the end of the *Brahmacharya Ashrama*. In ancient times, students went to study in forest schools (*guru-kula*), where they were taught by men equipped with the power of renunciation and asceticism.

The teachers were *vanaprasthis* who had renounced their household responsibilities and had dedicated their lives to pursuit of the spiritual goal—Self-realization. At the same time, they taught students in the spirit of Karma Yoga (actions performed for purifying the heart).

The students received academic knowledge to help them with the practical aspects of their life, and at the same time they acquired insight into the *Vedas*, which promoted their spiritual evolution. They received knowledge in two aspects: *apara vidya* (lower or academic knowledge) and *para vidya* (higher knowledge) that leads to liberation. In the process they were also influenced by the loving care and wisdom of the wife of their *guru*, whom they considered as their mother.

Time to Serve Society

After they had completed their studies, they received special blessings from their guru. In turn they gave gifts to their guru. They were now ready to marry and enter *Grihastha Ashrama* and become an active member of society.

It is important to note that when a student returns from the forest school *(guru-kula)* he has not completed his entire education. He has to go on receiving education in different ways. However, he becomes an active member of society. He begins to perform some job, or take up some profession so that he can help his family and contribute to the good of society.

In modern education, however, there is a serious defect. Students continue to receive education for many years, during which time they do not do anything practical for their family and society. The ancient ideal was to give a student an ethical basis for his life and endow him with sufficient skill and learning so that he may become useful to his family and society. This is a matter that today's social leaders need to reflect upon.

THE SAMSKARA OF MARRIAGE

If one has been properly disciplined during the student stage of life, the *grihastha* or householder stage will be delightful and fulfilling. There will be maturity of understanding. A life that is not based on discipline and order is like a house without foundation.

Enlightenment—Not Pleasure—Is The Goal

Marriage in Hindu Dharma was not designed to give license to the instinctive pleasure urge that abides in every human being. All living beings have the biological urge of procreation, but as a human being you have the capacity and possibility of attaining liberation. Keeping this in view, the *Vedic* culture gives a direction and meaning to the sex-urge through the sacrament of *Vivaha.*

It should be understood that sexual intimacy between husband and wife becomes a source of greater pleasure when it is viewed as a means to the unfoldment of deeper love—a love that brings unity of the mind, the heart and the soul.

Bhoga Vritti Degrades

In the modern world, it is considered by many to be a mark of "progress" that people can indulge in sexual intimacy freely, without any restriction, without any sense of shame. But in reality it is not so. True progress or freedom does not lie in becoming a slave to the uncontrolled senses, nor does it lie in giving sanction to every urge for passion and pleasure.

If *bhoga vritti* (pleasure-desire) dominates the mind, there is no room for adjustment between husband and wife; there is no patience. The moment a desire is thwarted, the moment there is frustration, the husband or wife wants to walk out of the marriage relationship— or they continue to live together in a state of constant dissatisfaction, each thinking that he or she could have been placed in a better condition. If pleasure becomes the main concern in a culture, society becomes fragmented—families lose their sense of stability and harmony, and the children that come from that type of shallow relationship are undisciplined and degenerate.

The Vedic Ritual of Jaya-Homa

The *Vedic mantras* are recited so that the bride and bridegroom may overcome all obstacles and attain victory in life. The essence of the *mantras* is given below:

"May my mind be full of knowledge. May I gain willpower. May I perform my duties with reflection and devotion. May I possess an unwavering mind. May I be endowed with discrimination so that I may realize the Truth. May my senses be healthy and strong. May my life be permeated with the spirit of *yajna* (sacrifice) and may it be filled with the songs of *Sama Veda* (harmony and peace)."

Vedic Ritual of Sapta-Padi

In the Hindu tradition, the bride and bridegroom go through an elaborate performance of rituals. Each ritual is accompanied by the chant of *Vedic mantras*, and has a deep mystical implication. The most important ritual is *sapta-padi*, which means taking seven steps.

The bride and bridegroom take seven steps around the fire. Keeping the Fire God as witness, they affirm their love for each other. The bride wishes the husband to be prosperous, endowed with food, strength, wealth, happiness, cows and other animals (the symbols of ancient prosperity), and agreeable conditions for every season. The bridegroom states in the seventh step: "We have walked together seven steps. We have become close friends. Let our love be abiding. May we together be united in profound love and perform our duties for the well-being of family, society and the world."

The Mysticism of the Seven Steps

Fire is the symbol of intuitional knowledge—the knowledge that confers liberation from the cycles of birth and death. Bride and bridegroom are reminded of the spiritual goal of liberation. It is for the accomplishment of the goal that they have joined their hands together.

There are seven Stages of Knowledge (*Jnana Bhumi-kas*). Each step symbolizes an ascent on the path of wisdom. The seven stages are: aspiration (*shubhechha*), reflection (*vicharana*), attenuation of desires (*tanumanasi*), enlightenment (*sattwapatti*), dispassion (*asamsakti*), negation of the world-process (*padarthabhavana*), and establishment in the transcendental Self (*turiya*).

SUCCESS IN MARRIAGE

In a successful marriage, husband and wife must help each other to unfold their full potential. The two souls that the Divine Plan has brought together must reciprocate in a process leading to the attainment of the four purposes of life: ethical perfection *(dharma)*, material prosperity *(artha)*, joyous family life *(kama)*, and liberation *(moksha)*.

If Self-realization is kept as the goal of life, there will evolve the best type of harmony and love in the family. However, if this goal is not kept in view, love will degenerate into delusion. And married life, instead of promoting freedom of the soul for both of the marriage partners, becomes a source of misery and bondage.

No Superiority or Inferiority

There should be no sense of superiority or inferiority between husband and wife. If the husband demands the right to be constantly dictatorial and thwarts the growth of the personality of his wife because of his ego, he is not following the path of righteousness.

In many families, the husband treats his wife just like a puppet, requiring that she behave exactly according to his ideas. That is a degrading situation. In an atmosphere of tyranny and submissiveness nothing good can grow. When the husband's negative qualities are never opposed, his vanity goes on growing with time, and the wife's weakness develops into a subservient nature.

Rather, there should be an atmosphere of genuine freedom in marriage in which one is not afraid of holding onto what one understands to be true. To establish such an atmosphere of freedom, it is important that householders understand the big psychological difference between humility and humiliation, between being humble and being submissive.

Under certain circumstances, a wise husband or wife will know that they are right about something, but will choose with humility to wait in expressing his or her opinion until a more opportune moment. In this manner, they maintain harmony without giving up their views or insulting their intellect.

To blindly accept and follow the wishes and dictates of your marriage partner when you are in disagreement with those wishes is building a relationship on a shallow basis. You cannot live in peace by going against your own understanding. There must be an environment of mutual freedom in which both personalities must evolve; and in that congenial atmosphere, their children will grow to be the best of men and women.

The Ideal Family

The ideal family is like a spring garden. When you enter the home, you sense the atmosphere of harmony and joy. According to the scriptures, an ideal family is blessed with the following:

Asha (optimism): Everybody's face is full of hope for a joyous future. There is hope towards the unknown and unexpected. When you develop faith in God, you know that every situation that is to come is for your spiritual advancement. Then the unknown always gives you a thrill. If you know exactly what is to happen, life becomes boring. So in a healthy family, there is a sense of joy with relation to the future.

Pratiksha (waiting with patience): This quality is a blend of perseverance with patience. Whatever project you adopt, you do your duty well, and then wait and watch with a deep inner conviction that success is yours. The Divine Hand is guiding you.

Sangata (good company): You draw to your home ideal friends and well-wishers, and avoid the company of those who are uncultured. In addition you set apart a time every day when all the family members may come together for a brief *satsanga* (good association). At times you may invite your neighbors to join in. The *satsanga* may be conducted with prayer, *kirtan,* a brief recitation from the scriptures, or a well planned study of the *Ramayana, Mahabharata, Bhagavata, Gita, Bible* or any scripture of your choice. You may conclude *satsanga* with *arati* and distribution of *prasad* (sacred food).

Sukarma (righteous actions): You perform special actions for the good of people around you. In an ideal family, every one is taught to amass the wealth of meritorious deeds.

Dana (charity): Perform acts of charity and generosity. You may share your wealth, your knowledge, your talents for the good of others. The spirit of charity does not depend upon your material attainments. You may not be rich, yet you can bring the light of hope where there is the darkness and despair. You can infuse patience and courage in others. Dissemination of knowledge is the highest form of charity.

Atitthya (hospitality): Be hospitable to people who visit your home. You are serving God in every guest that comes to you.

The Spirit of Yoga

In daily life, perform your duties—no matter what they may be, no matter how big or small—in the spirit of Karma Yoga, considering every action as an offering to God. Whether you are attending to your child, doing household chores, balancing your budget, adapting and adjusting in relationships—perform those tasks in the spirit of Karma Yoga. View your life as a grand opportunity for worshipping God in various ways. This is the secret for an enduring relationship that is blessed with peace, prosperity and harmony.

See the Divine in Each Other

Every husband should develop the attitude that it is the *Devi* (the Goddess) who abides in his wife, and thus he should adore her. And every wife should feels that it is God (as Krishna or Rama or any other manifestation) who is being worshipped in her husband. The scriptures say, *"Yatra Naryastu Pujyante Ramante Tatra Devata"*— "Where women are worshipped, there the Gods rejoice."

The attitude of worship in a broad sense implies a profound reverence for the soul of each other. With this attitude, there evolves an ideal love—a love that sacrifices, that waits with patience, that is ever intent upon being helpful and compassionate. Such a love is not thwarted by adverse conditions of life; rather, like the moon it shines brighter and brighter as the clouds of adversity pass on.

Seeing and worshipping God in each other creates a sublime setting for a secure marriage. In such an environment there is no dread of disharmony. That type of family is like a tree that can allow itself to be shaken violently in wind, yet does not break. Husband and wife can openly quarrel, openly express their views without feeling that they are shaking their inner foundation of unity and love.

The Hindu Ideal

According to the Hindu ideal, husband and wife are enjoined to be true and faithful to each other. That sexual fidelity promotes a deeper unity and enhances the spiritual well-being of the family. Also, according to the Hindu ideal, marriage is indissoluble. Husband and wife become loving companions for life—with the wish that if the bondage of *karma* has not dissolved at the time of death, they might continue to be companions in future lives as well.

However, under certain unusual marital conditions, Hindu tradition allows for *apat dharma*—duty in exceptionally distressing situations. If husband and wife are extremely ill-matched, if the husband batters his wife, or the wife torments her husband without any reason or rhyme, then nothing material or spiritual can be gained out of that union. Orthodox people may still insist that they should continue to stay together for the pride of the family and for maintaining the old tradition, but in the light of truth, it would be better if they separated, and lived their lives without the constant conflict, mental torture and degradation.

This however does not imply that a person should continue to marry and divorce, led by his whims. A marriage should not be broken up simply because there are impediments. Rather there must be a deeper love that transcends impediments. Keeping the spiritual purpose of life always in view, adjustments must be made—with love, understanding, self-restraint, adaptability and sacrifice—to maintain stability in the marriage.

Every Situation Is Helpful for Your Evolution

There was a saint whose wife was always bitter and quarrelsome. No matter what he did, there was always turmoil at home. Instead of finding fault with her, he used to say, "O God, how great you are that you have given me a wife who continues to inspire *vairagya* (dispassion) in my heart. She always reminds me that this world is imperfect. I do not have to go to an *ashram* to acquire *vairagya*—I can get it right here!"

Socrates had that type of wife. One day when Socrates was talking to his disciples, his wife was shouting a lot. He turned to his disciples saying, "Thundering clouds seldom rain." After awhile, however, she dumped some garbage on his head and he turned to his disciples again and said, "Well, I suppose that sometimes thundering clouds do rain!" He viewed all that happened in his marriage in a dispassionate way.

There was another saint whose wife was loving, sweet and ever ready to please her husband. The saint used to thank God, saying, "O God, You are so merciful that You have given me a wife who is so agreeable and loving. She encourages me at all times and keeps me free from worries so that I can devote myself to You."

The dispassionate vision of these saints teaches you that when you turn to the goal of Self-realization, you view every situation as helpful towards the attainment of that goal. In other words, your mind should not nurture the strong egoistic concept: "If I had been married to someone else, I would have been much better off." That is a big illusion. No matter what the personality of your spouse may be, there is a meaning behind the relationship. Further, with spiritual insight, you may bring about a great transformation in your husband or wife. Divine Love conquers all obstacles.

HARMONY IN HUMAN RELATIONS

The mansion of human progress and prosperity depends upon the foundations of harmony at home and in society. Just as lotuses bloom in the silent hours of the night, so do Divine qualities in a person bloom in the gentle hours of harmony and peace.

The world is a manifestation of the Supreme Being, God. Unity underlies all diversity. Just as innumerable waves are sustained by the same ocean, so too are innumerable beings sustained by the same Immortal Self, the Lord of all hearts. All human beings have the same Spirit that sustains them. Therefore, however varied others may be in their tastes and temperaments, our dealings with them should be based on a vision of unity.

God is not as pleased by chants of praise or utterances of prayers as by acts and deeds conducive to harmony and happiness in the family and society. More love and less hatred, more forgiveness and less impatience, more persuasion and less force should be the characteristics of a life that breathes in unity and harmony.

Human relations are often superficial. Once a deaf man went to see an old friend in the hospital. The friend was seriously ill. He was counting his days. The deaf man knew that he could not hear his friend talk, and since he didn't want his old friend to know that he had become deaf, he planned in advance a conversation that he was sure would be a comfort to the sick man.

He first asked, "Are you all right my friend?" "I am getting weaker every day," replied the patient. The deaf man, thinking his friend was getting better, said, "Thank God, I am so pleased to hear this." The sick man was terribly hurt. He thought this man was wishing him ill and he became annoyed.

The deaf man asked again, "What food have you eaten today, my friend?" The patient angrily replied, "Poison!" "May you have good digestion," the deaf man replied. The patient was fuming. He told his friend to leave at once, and had him removed. The deaf man departed with a smiling face, unaware of his friend's situation.

Being too concerned with the noises of their own minds, people do not try to understand others. They are deaf to others' problems. Such inability to understand others leads to various forms of disharmony in our daily relations. When disharmony creeps into a family, every word and action of each member is misunderstood. It is only when harmony breathes over their agonized hearts that they are able to regain their health, thereby allowing their blisters of bitterness to be healed.

Adapt and Adjust

Adapt and adjust. Do not develop egoism, pride or arrogance. A little act of humility and submissiveness can often bring great rewards. There is a parable in the

Mahabharata that illustrates this point. Once the Ocean asked the River Ganga, "Oh Goddess Ganga, you always bring me mighty trees, but you have never brought me any of those canes and reeds that grow abundantly on your banks. Why is that?"

The River Goddess replied, "Oh Lord, the trees are unbending and hard-hearted. That is why they are up-rooted by me. But the canes and reeds are humble and adapt to changing conditions. When my impetuous currents sweep over them, they bend down, humbling themselves. Thus, my strength is nullified and they remain unaffected. When the floods pass away, the canes and reeds rise again. It is due to their adaptability and humility that they are not destroyed."

Similarly, those who have not learned the art of adapting and adjusting to people around them are broken-hearted when adversities come. But those who can adapt are unaffected. Therefore, do not build up tension with others over mere trifles. Life is short. Try to enjoy this glorious gift of God—your life and its possibili-ties—by developing an expansive heart.

Curb Negative Imagination

Often, negative imagination becomes a great cause of disturbance and disharmony. Sri Ramakrishna told the following parable about the power of imagination:

Once there was a man lying by the road. A thief passed by and concluded, "This man has fallen because he could not sustain the heavy booty that he stole last night." When a drunkard passed by, he mumbled, "This man has had too much to drink!" A Saint then passed by and said, "This man is so immersed in God that he has lost his body-consciousness. How glorious!"

Even so, one judges external conditions on the basis of one's thoughts and imaginations. Try to rise above the limitations of imagination to perceive things as they really are. When someone does not greet you, do not imagine that he has become your enemy. When you have a slight cold, do not imagine that you are suffering from pneumonia. When you have a slight difficulty with your wife or husband, do not imagine that the two of you will never see harmony again. Check negative imagination in order to live happily.

God Is the Reality Behind All

Feel that all relationships are manifestations of *karma*—the results of actions performed in the past. Do not expect too much from others. No relation is permanent and secure. In the turbulent waters of the world-process, God is the only reality which is solid as a rock. Love God in all. True and abiding love is different from attachment and infatuation. Love your near and dear ones, but do not become attached to them. Attachment is the cause of worry, grief and frustration. Love the Lord in all. Serve the Lord in all.

Do not speak harsh words to anyone, because the Lord indwells all hearts. Do not harm anyone in thought, word or deed. No matter how inimical a person may be, one should not try to harm him. This is the practice of nonviolence.

In the Hospital of the World-Process

Those who do wrong deeds based upon jealousy, greed and pride are like patients. Their problems are not solved if you harm or destroy them. A disease should be cured, and killing the patient is not the correct method of curing the disease. Even so, cruelty, hatred, pride and jealousy are diseases of certain human beings. They should not be harmed, but their diseases should be treated.

Often, one is eager to give advice to others. But advising others is a great art. No one should force others to give up their wrong ways of thinking and feeling; they must rather be persuaded by love. Be an example yourself. Be a source of inspiration for others.

Harmony in Bringing Up Children

Do not spoil your children with too much attachment, indulgence and infatuation. Children are not mere toys for you to play with. They are souls working their way through their human forms. It is your duty to impart true education to them—to bestow on them proper conditions for both their secular studies as well as spiritual studies which lead to the understanding of the deeper values of life.

Mix affection with firmness in order to bring up your children properly. Train and discipline them so that they may become broad-hearted and serviceable to humanity. In this way they will develop aspiration to realize God.

Let there be harmony between husband and wife.
Let there be harmony between parents
and their children.
Let there be harmony among different relatives.
Let there be harmony among friends.
Let there be harmony among nations.
Let there be harmony among the elements.
Let there be harmony between the earth and the sky.
Let harmony be experienced everywhere!

May God bless you with harmony and peace!!

Goddess Saraswati—The Embodiment of Wisdom

3

AUSTERITY AND YAJNAS

Grihastha Ashrama
is a field for
very intense austerity
towards spiritual advancement.
It depends upon the angle of vision:
Once you change the angle from
Bhoga to Moksha—
from sense-pleasure to liberation—
your life becomes a stream
of prayer and austerity
that will lead you
to the highest.

AUSTERITY THAT LEADS YOU TO THE HIGHEST

As I have pointed out to you, *Grihastha Ashrama* is the backbone of society. All those who belong to the other three *Ashramas* (orders of society)—*Brahmacharya* (students), *Vanaprastha* (those who are retired), and *Sanyasa* (those who have taken to the order of renunciation)—depend upon the householders.

If householders are not well-disciplined, society will not have disciplined students; it will not have mature aged people who can guide others, and there will be no spiritual teachers. Therefore the responsibility of *Grihastha Ashrama* is of immense importance.

The Story of Kaushika Brahmin

The scriptures highlight the glory of *Grihastha Ashrama* as a training ground for the highest attainments in life—an opportunity to practise austerity of the greatest merit. The *Mahabharata* tells the story of a *brahmin* called Kaushika who practised intense austerities in a forest. One day, while in deep meditation, he was disturbed by a bird who let fall its droppings right on his head. He looked up in anger, and the bird was burnt up. Due to the practice of austerity, he had generated psychic power which caused the destruction of the bird. When he saw what happened to the bird, he developed a spiritual pride that he had attained perfection in his *sadhana* (spiritual discipline).

After a little while he went out to get alms from the nearby village and he knocked at the door of a house-holder. A lady came forth and said, "O venerable *brahmin*, please wait; I will give you something." Saying this, she went back into her house, and due to some development that came up in her household, forgot all about the *brahmin* waiting at the door. After quite some time, her husband came home, and she began to attend upon him. While doing so, she suddenly remembered the ascetic at the door. Feeling regret for the delay, she quickly brought the food for the *brahmin*, saying, "Please forgive me for taking such a long time to serve you." The *brahmin* merely looked at her with great sternness. She said, "O *brahmin*, please don't think that I am the bird that flew over you in the forest. I can't be burnt up like that!"

Kaushika was surprised, and asked, "How did you know of that incident? There was no one around." She replied, "In the performance of my duties for my family, I have gained special powers." Kaushika asked, "How can it be possible that a *grihasthi* can attain psychic powers without practising intense austerities—while living comfortably at home? You have not practised austerities, and yet you were able to tell what happened to me in the forest."

The lady replied, "I do not have time to spare, I have a lot to do. However, you may go to a spiritual person who is a butcher—Dharma-Vyadha (Righteous-Butcher) by name—who will give you the answer."

So, out of curiosity, the *brahmin* Kaushika travelled a long distance to find the village where the butcher dwelt. He was intrigued by the idea that he could learn something from a low-class butcher.

When he reached the village, he found Dharma-Vyadha engaged in weighing the meat and selling it to people. The butcher, having seen him from a distance, said, "O yes, I know someone has sent you here. Please wait." After he finished his job he took the *brahmin* to his home and there he gave him an elevating spiritual teaching. He taught him that austerity is not confined to some disciplinary practice. Greater austerity is practised by householders when they have to adjust day by day to so many demands. When they continue to perform their duties even in the midst of difficult situations, they acquire the merit of having performed great austerities.

Austerities of a Householder

If a *brahmachari* (a bachelor student) were to keep awake on a vigil for one night, he would be so proud, feeling as if he has performed a great austerity. A *grihasthi*, however, sometimes keeps awake night after night. If a child cries, if the roof leaks, if a certain problem demands his attention—he performs his duties without developing any spiritual pride.

So one must understand that *Grihastha Ashrama* is a field for very intense austerity towards spiritual advancement. It depends upon the angle of vision. Once you change the angle from *bhoga* (sense-pleasure) to *moksha* (liberation), your life becomes a stream of prayer and austerity that will lead you to the highest.

As you change that angle of vision, you will not feel a sense of contradiction between householder life and spiritual *sadhana*. Many *grihasthis* feel that since they are householders it is not possible for them to follow the spiritual path in an intensive manner. Many feel that modern society, with all its rush and tension, puts such a demand on their time that there is no time left to practise Yoga. "How can there be liberation for a *grihasthi?*" they ask. "If I were not a householder, I would have lived in a forest and concentrated all my energy on attaining enlightenment." But this is a layman's concept, and it is fraught with error. Nothing could be further from the truth.

All the tasks you do with the correct angle of vision are *sadhana*—spiritual discipline leading you to the highest goal: God-realization. If a householder is performing his duties with faith, devotion and insight, then he is in a better situation than many of the *brahmacharis* (celibates) and *Sanyasis* (those belonging to the order of renunciation) who have turned away from *Grihastha Ashrama* due to sentimental reasons. If a person adopts the order of renunciation without having a mature basis for his choice, he is less likely to advance than a sincere and introspective householder.

If you live in a spiritual center performing certain duties, you may develop a sense of great achievement within yourself. A *sanyasi* living in an *ashram*, having read a few books of *Vedanta* philosophy, and having practised some spiritual discipline, may suddenly develop the idea that he has attained a great height, that he has mastered anger and passion, that he has conquered his mind. He begins to look down upon others. This spiritual pride becomes the greatest obstacle to his spiritual growth.

On the other hand, because householders are being put to test day by day, it is harder for them to develop such crippling spiritual pride. If a *grihasthi* develops the conceited notion one morning after prayer that he has conquered anger in his personality, the chances are that by nightfall, after being continuously tested by the demands of others around him, he will again lose his temper—as well as his false pride!

The scriptures have given many examples of enlightened *grihasthis*. King Janaka was a householder and a great king. In spite of this, he was a fully enlightened Sage.

Thus, it should be remembered that every *ashrama* (stage in life) has its own dignity and value—and can lead a sincere aspirant to the highest. Every situation in which you are placed has evolved out of a *karmic* law, backed up by the Divine Plan. The infinite intelligence of God is behind it. Therefore, do not complain about your circumstances. By complaining, you accomplish nothing. But, if you utilize every situation with a relaxed mind, it begins to unfold its spiritual purpose. It becomes a part of your *sadhana* (spiritual discipline).

Sadhana for a Householder in the Modern World

The problems posed by the modern world have to be viewed and tackled by a mature mind. Such a mind is not steeped in orthodoxy, but is ready to understand the true spirit of *dharma* (religion).

Fill Your Days with Integral Yoga

If you want to grasp the true spirit of the Hindu religion in a brief and precise manner, study the *Gita*. The *Gita* gives you the best guidelines. The *Gita* teaches that in everyday life, one should perform one's duties, no matter what they may be, in the spirit of Karma Yoga— with the understanding that by your actions you are worshipping God. By doing so your heart is purified. Gradually you become free of anger, hatred, greed, passion and other impurities of the lower self.

As you perform your actions in this manner, you begin to develop devotion to God. Devotion endows you with a peaceful mind. You begin to advance in meditation. Meditation leads to the unfoldment of wisdom— which enables you to realize, "I am not this perishable personality; I am the Immortal Self." Thus, in daily life, there should be a blend of performance of one's duty (Karma Yoga), devotion (Bhakti Yoga), meditation (Dhyana Yoga or Raja Yoga), and wisdom (Jnana Yoga).

Adopt An Attitude of Constant Worship

When a husband feels that it is the *Devi* (Goddess) who is being worshipped in his wife, and the wife feels that it is God who is being worshipped in her husband, and both feel that it is the Divine Krishna who is being brought up as a child in their family, then all relationships become a constant worship of the Divine Self. You are worshipping God from morning till night, no matter how busy you are.

Overcome the Negative with the Positive

Situations that present themselves before you may be agreeable or disagreeable, sweet or bitter. Both are needed in life, and must be well utilized. If they are bitter, turn your mind to God and you will find a way to make the bitterness go away. But do not handle bitterness by bitterness. Do not handle negative with negative.

For example, suppose one of the marriage partners does something wrong. The other person should not try to excel his partner by doing something even worse! If the husband stays angry for a day, the wife should not plan to stay angry for two days. That kind of attitude is absolutely wrong.

The first impulse in everyone is always "a blow for a blow." The moment someone acts negatively, the immediate urge is to act negatively right back. But a greater fulfillment of your deeper nature lies in cultivating patience and insisting on goodness. No matter how many times you may fail, you must exercise your goodness, your love, and your understanding to overcome the negative aspect of your partner's personality.

Practise Introspection

A great art that a householder must learn is introspection. Introspect, but introspect without sentimentality and with great perseverance.

Every day you must wash your dirty dishes. If a dish needs scrubbing today, you do not sit back and think: "Today I'm scrubbing the dish and tomorrow it will be dirty again. So why should I clean it? Why not bang it and break it?"

Much in the same manner, look into your mind day by day, without sentimentality, to see how it must be "scrubbed up." When you see the errors in your personality, in your life, resolve to correct them. Do not think: "The same problem will repeat itself again and again. There are so many things to be adjusted. It is impossible to change anything." Little by little, practise introspection and try to correct whatever error you see. God is within you. By His Grace you can accomplish amazing changes within yourself and in others—you can promote harmony and peace in your family as well as among people around you.

THE FIVE GREAT YAJNAS

According to the *Vedic* scriptures, a householder should perform five *yajnas* or sacrifices. A *yajna* is a purificatory action—a course of action that helps one to be free of the impurities of the mind, such as passion, anger, greed, hatred and others. It is as if you have kindled a mystic fire in the altar of your heart, and you pour your impurities into that fire.

Deva Yajna

The first is called *Deva Yajna,* which means worshipping God. You may worship God as Rama, Krishna, Vishnu, Shiva, Devi, or as *Brahman,* or in any manner according to your faith. Worship implies meditation, prayer, repetition of *mantra* (a Divine name or mystic formula), and surrender to God.

The aspect of God that you choose for your worship is called your *Ishta Devata* (your chosen Deity). For example, if you have chosen Rama as your *Ishta Devata,* you meditate upon Lord Rama, and repeat the *mantra*— *"Om Sri Ramaya Namah."*

It is important to understand that God is One. However, He may be meditated upon and worshipped in various ways. The various Gods and Goddesses of the Hindu religion are essentially manifestations of One *Brahman* (the Absolute Self).

Lord Krishna says in the *Gita*:

"May you satisfy the gods by performance of sacrifice. In turn, may the gods, thus satisfied, enhance your fulfillment. Thus assisting each other may you attain the highest good in the form of Self-realization." (Ch.3-11)

A life that is not permeated by the spirit of sacrifice is meaningless. Lord Krishna says, "Those good people who eat only what is left from the sacrifice are freed from all sins. But those evil men who prepare food for themselves alone are eaters of sin." (Ch.3-13)

The implication is that when you live your life for the satisfaction of your ego, or for the sake of sense-enjoyments alone, your consciousness continues to contract. You become self-centered. And through this process you are plunged in increasing darkness (ignorance).

But when you learn to dedicate your actions, thoughts, feelings, and enjoyments to the Indwelling God within you, you begin to follow the path of Light. Your consciousness expands and your personality is decked with the fragrant flowers of Divine virtues.

By performing *Deva Yajna*, not only do you experience increasing inner joy, but at the same time you contribute to the happiness, peace and prosperity of the world in a mysterious way.

Rishi Yajna

Sages have given a vast store of knowledge in the form of scriptures. That scriptural knowledge, which is a treasure of immeasurable value, is the heritage of every human being. However, much of the *Vedic* wisdom has not yet been explored and very little has been introduced to people.

Humanity at large is not aware of the great treasure that lies in the Hindu scriptures. There is a great wealth of knowledge related to psychology and parapsychology in *Raja Yoga Sutras*. There are profound insights and practical techniques for integrating one's personality to be found in scriptures dealing with Jnana Yoga (Yoga of wisdom), Bhakti Yoga (Yoga of devotion), Raja Yoga (Yoga of meditation), Karma Yoga (Yoga of action), and their numerous ramifications.

Rishi Yajna implies studying scriptures for gaining knowledge, and in turn, sharing knowledge with others. Adopting this practice, spiritually enlightened personalities become like research scholars. By their insight and experiences, by their example, thoughts, and writings, they continue to elaborate the scriptural teachings for generations to come.

Pitri Yajna

This form of sacrifice refers to performing special religious rites for pleasing the souls of the forefathers.

The spirits of forefathers are said to abide in a particular *loka* (astral plane) which is called *Chandra Loka* (the plane of the Moon). The "Moon" in this context does not refer to the physical moon; it is the mystic plane of subtle enjoyments.

The souls of the forefathers, due to their different states of spiritual evolution and their *karmas*, may abide in different subtle planes, and some of them may be liberated as well. Yet it is the duty of the householders to remember them and perform special worship, prayers and righteous actions for them.

From the ritualistic point of view, householders perform *shraddha* (offering of rice cakes) and *tarpana* (oblation). They do so on the anniversary of the day of death and also on every New moon-day. When this *Yajna* is performed with faith and devotion, the souls of the forefathers that are in hellish conditions receive upliftment, while the souls that are in heavenly conditions are led to further enrichment of their joys. They receive increased satisfaction, strength and nourishment.

Pitri Yajna in Modern Times

From a broader point of view, everything that you do in this world should enhance the fame and glory of your family and of your forefathers. You should conduct yourself in a way that would make your forefathers proud if they were here to see your actions and achievements.

As long as the souls are not liberated, there is still an interrelationship between you and the souls of your forefathers. If someone in a family does great, virtuous deeds, the forefathers rejoice in heaven. The scriptures say that if someone in the family line attains enlightenment, or becomes a saint or a sage, thereby he causes great upliftment in seven generations of forefathers.

A son is called *putra*, because his actions enable the souls of the forefathers to be free from the hellish world of *Puta*. The same is applied to a daughter, who is called *putri*. Due to limitation in understanding, people began to give more importance to sons than to daughters. This however is the result of ignorance. Either a son or a daughter will, by his or her righteous actions, bring delight to the souls of the forefathers.

It is the responsibility of everyone to keep up the pride of the family line by the performance of actions that promote the good of all. Only good actions and attainments can delight the forefathers. On the other hand, negative actions or sinful deeds are displeasing to the forefathers.

Nri Yajna or Manushya Yajna

This *Yajna* takes the form of righteous deeds performed for the good of other human beings. All acts of compassion—such as feeding the hungry, providing medical help to the sick, helping the aged, giving education to the illiterate, and relieving the manifold sufferings of humanity—are *Manushya Yajna* in the broad sense.

God dwells in all. When you promote love and understanding within your family and outside of your family with people around you, you are worshipping God in a special way. You are performing *Manushya Yajna*. By these acts of goodness you attain purity of heart.

The act of goodness should not be confined to your family and friends alone, but it should extend towards all human beings irrespective of differences due to cast, creed, nationality, faith, religion and sex.

Bhuta Yajna

This *Yajna* consists of your duties towards animals, birds, and lesser forms of life. People today are becoming more and more aware of the importance of every living creature. This is a world where plants, trees, animals, birds, fishes, insects and worms are all interrelated. They provide an ecological balance.

A special attitude of worshipping the cow has been evolved among the Hindus. The cow is chosen as a representative of all animals. Just as you show your gratitude to human beings for their acts of kindness, so too you need to show your gratitude, reverence and love for animals such as cows that give you milk and its numerous products to nourish your body. The idea of giving honor to cows is designed to lead your mind to the ideal of worshipping God in all beings.

In Hindu culture, certain trees such as the Peepal tree and certain herbs such as the holy basil are worshipped. The implication is to have reverence for all trees and plants, and not to damage vegetation without rhyme or reason.

In addition, on special days such as Naga Panchami (a sacred day for the Hindus), people bring milk and place it at the holes where snakes may abide. This is to worship the Self that dwells in snakes and cobras.

The Five Debts

Summarily, it is believed that everyone comes into this world with five debts he needs to pay. By worshipping God you pay your debt to the *Devas (Deva Yajna)*. By performing special rites and righteous actions in the name of the departed souls, you are paying your debt to the forefathers. By performing righteous and generous deeds to human beings, you are paying your debt to humanity. And by developing respect for life and helping animals and plants, you are paying your debt to the living beings who are in the lower scales of evolution.

The Ideal

The ideal is to understand that you are spiritually related to the entire universe. You are related to God Himself. In fact, you are essentially the Divine Self. In the process of repeated cycles of birth and death, you have passed through numerous embodiments—you have been trees, birds, animals, human beings. And by your good *karmas*, you may rise to the status of gods in the heavenly world. Thus, keeping this in view, this whole universe is your family.

Moving one step further, you worship the Divine Self in and through the creation by the performance of the five *yajnas*. Your are led to develop the cosmic vision that "This entire creation is My body. All beings are different parts of My own personality. I am the Self in all." When this vision develops, you become liberated from the cycles of birth and death.

Sri Swami Jyotirmayananda

4

EDUCATION

*To be educated,
in the more profound sense,
implies being able
to develop your human potential
and higher human values,
being able to handle your mental stress,
being able to live with people with adaptability,
developing the Divine qualities of the soul:
humility, goodness of the heart,
compassion, selflessness.
If these are lacking,
one is not educated.*

EDUCATING CHILDREN

The subject of educating children is a very vital subject because the future of mankind—culture, tradition, religion, all that is good and sublime—depends upon the way children are educated. Children grow up into adults and adults again become children in the process of the repeated cycles of birth and death based on *karma* and reincarnation.

Further, the test of a great culture is the art with which children are educated. If children stay frustrated in a society, if they undergo mental torture, if they are not given normal circumstances for higher development and for understanding what is good and what is evil, then such a society is in a state of degradation. It is important, therefore, to understand what type of attitudes parents must evolve towards their children, towards themselves and towards their mutual education.

A Karmic Relationship

One must have the philosophical understanding that children are spirits in the process of repeated embodiment and it is on the basis of the law of *karma* that parents draw certain souls within their family. So, a child's coming to a home is not an accidental development. It is backed up by a law. The spirit of the child needs an environment that will fulfill the demands of its *karma*. Accordingly, the parents have been arranged by nature's laws. So, in a way, the child is the father of the man. It is the soul of the child which selected the parents through whom it is born.

According to the Yogic thought, a child is learning even when he is within the mother's womb. Even then the child is receiving impressions. So, in Yogic culture an expectant mother is given an abundance of good association, *satsanga*. She is careful about where she goes, the thoughts she entertains in her mind, and even the pictures she sees. If she is always seeing the picture of Napoleon with his hands folded ready for battle, the child will probably develop those impressions. And so, according to Yogic culture, you can actually bring forth a child according to your liking. You can make a child a sage, a warrior, a politician, a skilled merchant, or a crooked thief.

On the other hand, you must realize you are not creating the child. The child has been drawn to you on the basis of *karma*. Whatever you do is in the fitness of the *karmic* law. At the same time this does not imply that you simply relax and follow your whims in the name of the law of *karma*. The law of *karma*, if properly understood, helps you to exercise your self-effort. Thus, you can control and take advantage of the laws of nature and promote goodness in yourself and others.

A Child Is a Reflection of the Self

Why is a child so lovable to the parents? How can a tiny creature weighing just a few pounds capture their hearts, entrance their minds and involve all their energy? Why is it that the moment you see a little cub of a tiger or a lion, or any baby from any species, the human mind develops such a sense of tenderness? What is the psychology behind it?

The answer, in brief, is that every human being wants to capture in his consciousness absolute tenderness, absolute beauty and harmony. That, of course, is God, the Divine Self. But since the urge for realizing the Self is very abstract, the complexed mind is unable to understand that urge and nature must present various experiences in human life to promote its development. So, when parents love their child, in that love they are trying to capture love of God. Your child reflects God in its simplicity and innocence.

When you understand how a child reflects your aspiration for becoming peaceful, symbolizing the goal you want to reach in life, you can develop an attitude of adoring the Divine Self in the child. This attitude however, should not interfere with your practical dealings with a child.

You must be able to separate your parental love from the objective needs of a child's growth. You should not make the child a toy in your hands, nor become attached to and dependent on the child for your happiness. If you do so you will stunt his development and not let him grow up as he should. Rather understand that a child exists as an independent personality and one day will walk out of your life just as a bird that has wings will fly out of its nest.

The Unique Sensitivity of the Child's Mind

A child, according to Yoga, has his kleshas, his afflictions, in a dormant state. Because the ego and its selfishness have not yet developed, there is a unique form of sensitivity which nature has given to a child.

In practical dealings with children, parents must understand the sensitivity of the child's mind and realize how deeply every experience penetrates that mind. You remember clearly many things from your childhood days while things that happened a few years or only a few days before are forgotten. The mind of a child is extraordinarily sensitive. Its sensitivity is mystic.

Sometimes the child is reflecting upon even the things that you feel and think. You may be able to conceal many things from other grownup human beings. You can come from your office tense, tired and filled with explosions within your mind. You can conceal all that when dealing with adults. But when you are sitting before tiny "sages"—your little children—they perceive your inner state though you have not uttered a word. There is a radiation from you that children are more sensitive to, and they imbibe it. So, it is important that adults consider carefully the sensitivity of the mind of a child.

See the World Through Your Child's Eyes

Parents must also understand how the values of children are different from the values of adults. There is a place of insight within you through which you can know how children feel, but most people have become rigid and do not remember childhood days. Those who are more integrated, however, do not grow rigid and they maintain an awareness of the child's reality.

So, it becomes important for parents to develop sensitivity and insight into children's psychology. Not through academic learning, but on the basis of spontaneous love and affection, you must become able to commune with your children and understand them. You must try to see how the children think and how they are looking at things—so that even though actions done by children are very fantastic, you will not upset them severely. You should not impose your realities in a very harsh manner in the tender environments of the children.

For example, a child in the the height of great sensitivity finds something he considers to be on the top of the world and he wants to show that to his mother. So, he brings a handful of mud and puts it right near her face. And all that he receives for that great act is one big slap!

Consider another illustration: Suppose you are a writer and as you are doing your work, your child sits and adores you for what you are writing. Then when it is time to go to the office, you leave. The child, in order to help you, sits down, takes all the ink and the pen and goes on turning all the pages, writing everywhere so that when you come back you will be so happy to see your work accomplished. You come back and the child is greeted by a volcanic eruption! So, it is important to see things from the child's point of view and not to hurt him because of his errors. Parents must understand the tender atmosphere in which children exist and must be able to appreciate their intentions in a sensitive manner.

A Place for All

The law of *karma* can cause great differences among children in the same family. Children born of the same parents may be in totally different levels of evolution. One can be a very saintly personality, another may be a demoniac personality. Some children have the potentiality of becoming very great in a particular field, while others do not. Parents with insight will be able to guide their children according to their evolution, encouraging them to unfold all their inner talents and resources. Parents should not become upset if the children do not function or develop the way that they had expected, because children have their own right to live and express themselves. They cannot be molded exactly according to the expectations of the parents.

The parent's attitude towards the children should be to present a healthy environment for growth, just as the sun and the rain provide a proper environment for seeds to grow. If the seed contains the potentiality of becoming a thorny bush, it grows into a thorny bush. If it contains the potentiality of becoming a rose, it grows into a rose. However, in proper perspective, even a thorny bush serves various medical purposes. Everything has its purpose.

If proper circumstances are given in a society where various personalities are needed, everyone will fit in to perform a correct and right function. From the Divine point of view no one is smaller, and no one is greater. Therefore, parents should not disbalance their affection and lean more towards children who are brighter or more like themselves and begin to ignore those that are not so bright or express themselves differently than the parents had expected.

The Spirit of Discipline

Practical insight into how to train children must be gradually developed by the parents through experience. There cannot be set laws. Those people who read set laws from research books become like tiny computers, constantly looking into the books to find out exactly how they are going to react to a problem.

Rather, there must be an inner feeling about the child brought about through vital communication. You may err many times and repent often for what you have done to a child. That too is a part of evolution.

Parents must build up an atmosphere of warmth and love, and within that atmosphere, firmness. Allow the children to taste the joy of your satisfaction when they have done well in meeting your healthy expectations. However, when they have not done something well, they must also taste the bitterness of having made you dissatisfied. They long to please you and learn to enjoy promoting your satisfaction. That sensitive way in which children must be handled is the subject of profound understanding and the art of being firm in a healthy manner requires a special intelligence.

You should not allow the child to have his way all the time. You must train and discipline the child—and your love for the child should not come in the way of that training. If a child gets into some wrong habits you must discipline him firmly, strongly. Even threats and little slaps will do no harm.

A story is given about a person who as a boy was not reprimanded by his mother when he started picking the pockets of others. Rather, the mother went on encouraging him and gradually he became a great criminal. Ultimately, he was sentenced for a long term imprisonment and at that time he asked to see his mother. When the mother came he put his mouth near her ear and bit it. The mother said, "Why did you do so?" He answered, "Why didn't you stop me when I first began this pilfering habit, this stealing? Why did you not stop me?"

So all the love the mother has shown according to her own confused understanding had turned into bitterness in her son's mind. Therefore, even though at the time of punishment it may seem to the child that you are not up to the mark of love, you must follow the ideal and the right process according to your capacity. The children will appreciate your actions in course of time.

Parents who fear that their children will leave them as they grow if they are firmly treated have not developed deeper love for the children. If you are in a healthy relationship with your children, you will impress upon them the sincerity of your intentions to such an extent that even though you might have punished them and been very harsh at times, they will love you immensely.

True Spiritual Education

Spiritual ideals should be given to children, but since people do not have a healthy understanding of the true meaning of spirituality, they often separate the spiritual from the material. Also, in their eagerness to train their children, parents generally err and, in the name of spirituality, impose their grossly frustrated personalities upon their children.

Therefore, you hear so much about cruelty that occurs when children are trained to become everything that the parents are not. Parents, finding in themselves many weaknesses that they cannot remove, want the child to be perfect, free from all those weaknesses. This type of attempt to build perfection in others without bringing perfection within oneself is an erroneous movement. Children are tortured, put into great trouble in the name of discipline, in the name of making them ethically perfect, training them to be pious, religious.

Religion is life—life lived in a healthy way. Religion is sincerity. Religion is communion with love. So, it is important not to adopt extreme measures in any direction and to provide conditions so that the children draw from themselves the inherent power with which they are born. That is exactly the meaning of education. Education is to draw out from yourself what you have.

To encourage aspiration for greater things, all you need to do is awaken an interest in the child. The moment a true interest is awakened, the child will follow that pursuit with intense concentration.

If a child develops an interest in Self-realization as the goal, he will start to read books that will help him reach that goal. Later when the child goes to school and starts studying other subjects you may become more concerned with practical realities and may say to the child, "Now, do not read the *Gita.* Do not read the *Upanishads* because they won't enable you to pass the examination. Read only your subjects." And you may even create various barriers for the child, yet he will find time without upsetting you to follow the pursuit if he has deep interest in it. Therefore, the art for parents is to plant in the child a profound interest, then leave the child to pursue it. Just guide here and there. Do not go after every detail.

For parents to present higher thought patterns in the environment of their children, certain conditions must be present. Firstly, the parents must have a higher understanding themselves and be sincerely working towards their own evolution and personality integration. Secondly, there must not be disharmony between the parents. Thirdly, the parents must not seek too many amusements outside. They should find time to be with their children—talking to them, playing with them, interacting with them. Children provide an excellent panorama of experiences for the parents. The parents, in turn, provide an interesting environment in which the personalities of their children can unfold.

Therefore, do not allow the children to just watch TV day and night. It is a terrible defect in the present civilization that parents leave the children completely at the mercy of mechanized entertainment and the children grow up cold, calculating and insensitive. Therefore, they bring pain to their parents and pain to the society.

Rather, come in contact with the children by telling them stories and parables. Participate in their lives and come closer to their world. Education is not limited to just training children how to read and write. Education is sharing your life, allowing a child to imbibe vibrations which are necessary for his growth.

As it has been pointed out to you before, bringing forth children is not merely an accidental development in the pursuit of pleasure, but, according to the Hindu tradition, is a powerful responsibility, a powerful Yoga. If that responsibility is not understood a person should not be a *grihasthi*, a householder, and bring forth children he is not prepared to deal with. On the other hand, if you learn the art of being a sincere and responsible parent, you are practising a most intense form of Yoga.

Your doing good to the child enables you, in turn, to evolve faster. You are not educating the child for the child's sake alone, but for your own sake as well. It is within the perspective of educating yourself that nature has provided a conjunction of a soul with you.

You must help bring out all the qualities that the child can unfold under your protection and guidance. When children bloom into wonderful personalities, when they turn towards life which is universal and truly healthy and when they become enlightened sages, they benefit themselves, the parents, the forefathers, and the entire world. That should be the goal of all education.

WHAT IS TRUE EDUCATION?

Education is meant to bring out your hidden talents, and to enable you to discover your essential nature and fulfill the purpose of your existence. In so doing you serve humanity in the best way possible. For the vast majority of people, however, the concept of education is extremely limited. People who have big titles or degrees from universities are recognized as educated people and, relatively speaking, that definition is perfectly correct. However, from the point of view of the ideological and philosophical understanding of education, that definition remains shallow. Simply having big degrees, a lot of recognition, and many titles does not imply that the person is educated in the true sense.

To be educated in the more profound sense implies being able to develop your human potential and higher human values, to be able to handle your mental stress, to be able to live with people with adaptability, to develop the Divine qualities of the soul: humility, goodness of the heart, compassion, selflessness. If these are lacking, one is not educated.

Let me relate to you a well known parable. Once a group of scholars entered a boat; one was a mathematician, another was a literary giant, another was a scientist. In the course of conversation, each asked questions of the boatman.

The mathematician asked him, "Have you ever read a treatise on mathematics, or have you had any experience with mathematics?" The boatman replied, "No. Just counting some mangoes and vegetables, but nothing beyond that." The mathematician said, "Then you have lost half of your life, since you have never had the joy and the thrill one experiences by possessing mathematical talent." The boatman felt miserable, and said, "What can I do? I was born in a poor family; I could never be educated."

Similarly, the scientist spoke about the wonderful strides taken in physics, in chemistry, in astronomy and in so many other branches of science. "Do you have any idea," he asked the boatman, "about the vastness of knowledge in science?" And the boatman said, "No. I am just a poor man." "Then you have lost a lot of your life; you've missed most of the joy of life."

And the literary man said, "Have you read Shakespeare or any other great poet? Have you experienced the joy of reading novels?" The boatman replied, "No. I have read nothing. I am illiterate." Now they all pitied him, and he himself felt very miserable.

But as the boat proceeded on its course through the river, it was caught by a whirlpool that tossed it from side to side. At this point the boatman said, "Do any of you know how to swim? Now we are in a difficult predicament and we may have to jump." And they all replied, "No, we do not know how to swim!" The boatman said, "Well, if that is the case, now all your life is gone!"

The moral of this story is that you may have extraordinary talents, you may be a computer expert, you may be a great mathematician, you may know how to erect a bridge or build a condominium, but when certain problems develop at home, can you handle them? When you suddenly hear something shocking—the doctor informs you that you have a terminal disease—what happens to your mental balance?

When some challenging situation actually develops in life, all your accomplishments do not come to your aid; then you feel as if you are drowning. On the other hand there are people who are not so educated from the academic point of view, but they can handle stressful situations, they can keep calm in adversity, they have mature judgment in difficult situations, they can advise others, and they radiate a sense of comfort and inspiration to others. Are not these people more educated than so many students that are being manufactured by so many universities year after year?

Educational System in Vedic Times

We must understand that the educational system, as it was in *Vedic* times, was geared to enable a student to serve himself and society. Therefore, it was founded on discipline. Anyone who entered the school had to follow the *Brahmacharya* order, which meant a complete discipline of the body, mind and senses.

In those times, every form of learning was called a *Veda*. If you were interested in martial arts you studied *Dhanur Veda*, and you learned archery under a *guru* who taught you *mantras* related to archery. First, he disciplined you well and then, when he found you qualified, he taught you archery. If you were interested in medicine you had to follow the disciplines of *Ayur Veda*. Every branch of knowledge was considered a *Veda*—which implied that whatever you were learning you learned with humility and with a spirit of serving God in humanity, always keeping in view the goal of life—Self-realization.

Education and the Four Purposes of Life

In order to understand education in its integral way, you should understand the four purposes of life: *dharma, artha, kama* and *moksha. Dharma,* or the cultivation of ethical values, is the basic purpose of life, and the foundation of education. All that you achieve and learn should be based on a sense of *dharma* or righteousness. You must possess a clear and sublime conscience. If *dharma* is not there, all your learning is in vain. If *dharma* is not there, all learning and accomplishment brings about a demoniac development. If a person who is undisciplined suddenly tumbles upon a great discovery, he may become a great man in the eyes of others; but, from a philosophical and spiritual point of view, if his discovery and his attainment become a source of misery for others, that is a demoniac achievement.

Therefore, education must have its roots in *Dharma*. The guiding line in an ideal educational system must be to promote harmony and goodness in people. One should never step beyond the principles of nonviolence, truth and purity. Greed, violence and passion must not be given license, but are to be controlled.

If a student starts his studies as a doctor, for example, with his mind set upon the idea, "One day I am going to be a millionaire and drive a Rolls Royce," then he is off to a poor start in the light of *dharma*. He may set up a wonderful dispensary or hospital and become quite wealthy, but when money is his main inspiration, the result is not the product of true education. Although that is the type of education that the majority of people are seeking now, it is not real education.

People crave pleasure, and pleasure seems to be the goal of the present educational process. Students dream of having lots of money, lots of power, the wealth to go anywhere they want and the resources to own anything they want. However, an education that caters to these values is not education, and an intellect that schemes for these things is called *bhoga buddhi*—intellect that wants only enjoyment.

There is an ancient saying from the *Mahabharata*: "*Sukharthinah kuto vidya*"—"There is no knowledge for one who loves comfort." If you are a lover of pleasure and comfort, there is no knowledge for you. You are not qualified for education. "*Kuto vidyarthinah sukam*"—"If you are a student, how can there be comfort?" There is no comfort for you if you truly seek knowledge. To shun comfort and luxury is not a miserable development, but rather a joyous development.

Imagine a student who is just twenty-five years old and wants his head propped up by a soft pillow on an easy chair; he doesn't want to do anything but move little buttons on a computer, and expects his parents to do all the heavy jobs at home. Outsiders observing the student may think he has become well-educated, but what type of person will he become later? Life presents so many threatening and challenging situations; if one has not been disciplined, if one is not accustomed to hard work, he is ill-prepared to face these challenges.

While teaching children one must not be overprotective and thus spoil the child. If a child is not accustomed to having his ego shaken a little, if he has not developed any patience and endurance in bearing insult and injury, he has not been cultivating *dharma* as the foundation of his education.

The second purpose of life is *artha*, or economic position. Money is a means to a higher end. Just having money does not mean anything at all. Observe how so many people gain millions of dollars overnight in the lottery, yet that doesn't make any difference in the deeper quality of their lives; all the defects in their personality can even become more exaggerated! This effect is similar to what happens when you look into a magnifying mirror: When there was no magnification, your face looked gentle and fine; but look into a strong magnifying glass and you become a giant and every hair looks like a big pole! That is what becoming suddenly rich can do—it does not in any way make you a better person.

On the other hand, if you are earning money with a basic grounding in *dharma*, then the money that comes to you becomes a means to your self-improvement, a means to helping society and performing good deeds. Used in this manner, it will not stir your vanity.

The next, and third, purpose of life is *kama*, or developing social relationships; that is also a part of education. If you cannot adapt and adjust with people, if you cannot have harmony with friends and family members, then life becomes empty.

No matter where you are or in what situation you are placed, you always find the challenge of different relationships. And if you cannot handle people with different moods and egocentricities, then life becomes empty. A person cannot live alone; even if you were in the Himalayas you will find that you are making friends with monkeys, birds or squirrels; you will find some relationship to overcome loneliness.

Kama is the value of life which allows you to live in harmony with others, so that you are then free to plan how you can help humanity. To be able to expand and outgrow one's ego is the most profound aspect of education. A truly educated person is inspired by compassion to help others, and he places every talent he has in service of others. In that way his talents increase more and more. Selflessness is the secret of discovering more and more talent and abundance within.

Moksha, or liberation, is the ultimate purpose in life. The entire educational process should lead you to liberation. In this stage the knowledge that you gain is known as *para vidya*. The *Upanishads* say there are two types of *vidya*, or knowledge: *apara* and *para*.

Apara is the lower knowledge or relative knowledge, the knowledge that helps you in your day to day life. And within that knowledge comes all the sciences, all the arts, all the subjects that are taught in universities. *Para vidya*, however, is the knowledge that is mystical. When you practise concentration and meditation and are guided by a guru, then you discover a knowledge which brings about a complete fulfillment of the urge to know. *Para vidya* is that knowledge by knowing which all is known.

Para vidya is the attainment in which all educational systems must culminate. That is the goal. Keeping this in view, an ideal student should develop self-discipline; he should strive to develop virtuous qualities like humility, patience, sincerity, and simplicity; he should practise self-introspection and austerity; he should be self-dependent; he should flow out of himself in service to humanity and thereby commune with God. These are the great highlights of true education. If you have these you are really educated. Anything other than this is a deviation—lack of education. May God bless you with the purity of intellect that leads you to the supreme knowledge or liberation!

TOWARDS INTEGRAL EDUCATION AND FREEDOM

Teaching is given in three ways: verbal, by example, and by influence. Talk to your children; but don't talk too much. Generally, parents overestimate the value of verbal teaching. One often hears, "Oh, I talked with my child for three hours. Everything is settled." Usually, nothing is settled; the next day things will be the same. Talking is good, but within measure. Rather, teach by your own example; start doing yourself that which you want the children to do.

The child receives impressions in a subtle way. You cannot hide anything from the child. So, if the parents are sincere and practising ethical values themselves, the child will imbibe it. If they are unethical, if they are in disharmony with each other, the child will imbibe that too. If you yourself are not perfect and you go on telling your children to behave perfectly, there will be problems. You yourself should be an example of what you teach.

If you ask your children to get up early in the morning, you must start doing so yourself. If you want them to keep things in order, set things in order yourself in your

own room. You can show them how you pick up everything, how you arrange things to save yourself a lot of
time, how you press clothes, how you wash the dishes,
how you put them away. After they have learned how to
do their chores, they will feel proud of doing those things
well.

Finally, by your own prayer and meditation you
project vibrations of goodwill: "May God grant our children keen intellect, better understanding, more health."
This is a subtle but powerful way in which you influence
your children.

Do Your Best—
But Remain Detached

In the worst situation, God is the best resolver. Turn
to God and realize that all this is a Divine Plan. People
and their destinies are not under your control. Sometimes, even the best of parents, due to some *karmic*
process, draw the worst of children.

But do your best according to your possibilities. You
may be the father in your family, but never feel that you
are The Father. The real father is The Father of all
fathers. Never think that you are handling the destinies
of your children. God is working through you in helping
the children. If that attitude is developed, then you do
your best and remain relaxed. If you have not developed
this attitude, then you suffer from guilt complexes about
how you have raised and educated your children, constantly lamenting, "If only I had been different..." In that
way you do not help yourself nor the child.

Academic vs. Spiritual Education

Education is of two types. One is academic education—education that will prepare your children to hold jobs, to earn money, to function in society—and the other is spiritual education. Spiritual education will prepare children to handle their sentiments and to handle their stress. Without this type of education, all other education becomes hollow.

Look at the people who are educated today. The majority of them do not know how to handle their ego when they are put into frustrating situations. There are millionaires, highly educated, whose living rooms and offices are filled with big titles that they have acquired through years of education. Yet the only solution they can find to their problems is to take a pistol and—BANG BANG!—kill themselves and all others around.

The Hindu religion has produced massive works that are profound psychological and spiritual texts, yet they seem like stories or fairy tales. Parents and children can read from the *Ramayana* or the *Mahabharata* or the *Bhagavata Purana* day by day. While these scriptures are easy to read and are highly entertaining, at the same time, they give lessons for handling temper, for outwitting the ego, for controlling the *gunas* (the modes of nature) that operate in your personality.

Provide Satsanga For Your Children

There are two types of *satsanga*: one type enables the children to do *puja* (worship), *japa* (repetition of *mantra*), prayer, Yoga exercises, and meditation, and the other teaches them the scriptures—such as the *Gita, Ramayana, Mahabharata.* Ideally you should have a prayer-room in your house, or a small shrine where you can come together for these forms of *satsanga.*

You and your children should come together for *swadhyaya* (study of scriptures) according to a schedule that fits the needs and interest of family members. The family could do this daily, twice a week, once a week, etc. As you study the scripture, one person may read and the others listen. A little discussion about what is read is healthy. You may hold this session for half an hour or more.

Relaxing Together in a Healthy Way

Learning the art of relaxation is of great importance for everyone. Family members should enjoy some wholesome form of exercise together. They can ride bicycles, go for a mile walk, go swimming in a lake—something that brings the family in contact with nature. In addition you should do some Hatha Yoga exercises. Gathering together for meals is an important time for family relaxation and communication. You should develop insight into *satwic* diet—vegetarian meals that are nourishing to you and your children.

Families can enjoy educational films together. Although most film entertainment is *rajasic* in nature and leaves the mind burdened, some special films bring good impressions. Expose the minds of your children to films such as the *Ramayana,* the *Ten Commandments* or other educational films that have been well done and convey a good message. By doing so you keep your children away from the influence of *rajasic* and *tamasic* films—films that are laden with passion and violence.

Kindle Spiritual Aspiration In The
Heart of Your Child

In the *Vedic* culture, before one is initiated into the student stage *(Brahmacharya Ashrama)*, he is given *Mundana Samskara*—shaving of the hair. Shaving is a reminder of the ultimate goal—sanyasa or renunciation—through which, one day, you shave off the entire world. Therefore this sacrament is like a mini-sanyasa, a small step towards the highest goal. It teaches the young student that his life must lead to the attainment of liberation.

Such traditions convey a powerful message to children. By performing this majestic sacrament, instead of telling your child, "You are here to serve this family, to bring pride to this family; you belong to us," you tell him, "O child, you belong to God. Your primary duty is to love God and serve Him." At the same time you are fully aware that when your child turns his steps to God, he will become a source of boundless blessings for the family and society.

Do not wait until your children have grown up to introduce them to the higher purpose of life. Rather, whether they understand it or not, perform *samskaras*, bring them into *satsanga* or good association, and kindle the lamp of spiritual aspiration even from their very childhood.

Educate the Ego to Be Satwic

Through the ego you are led to evolve; through the ego you guide others. When you guide your children you do so through their ego. When you tell your children how wonderfully they have done, and the children begin to expect your appreciation, led by their ego they start working harder.

Although nature has planned that things are done through the ego, ultimately, when your ego becomes extremely *satwic* (pure), you experience profound humility. You are ever aware of the fact that you are merely an instrument in Divine Hands. Thus, you go beyond the ego.

If, led by your ego, you continue performing good deeds, ego is gradually reduced. But when you do negative deeds, ego becomes intensified. Ego becomes reduced when there is *sattwa* (purity) in the mind. If you do *rajasic* things (actions based on anger, hate, falsehood, etc.) then ego becomes intensified. Your evolution and the evolution of your children depend upon the way ego is handled.

Gifts of Spirit Excel Those of Matter

Instead of spending time and interacting with their children, parents often give gifts of money, cars, watches, etc. to show their affection. That is a terrible mistake. A family should provide vital associations. It is not so much money and external glamour, but a vital atmosphere that gives something precious to an individual that he cannot get elsewhere.

The best gift that parents can give their children is their company. Sit with your child, talk, share. Make the child so confident that the child can open up his or her heart to you. In such an atmosphere there is a mutual blessing.

When you see your child expressing himself openly, with trust, there is a feeling of fulfillment. And in turn, you can then help your child in the best way possible. When there is real communication, each family member learns about the problems of the others and helps them to handle those problems. But when your relationship consists of just giving and receiving in an external and materialistic way, then the relationship remains shallow. People try to take advantage of each other rather than to help each other. Children wait until the parents go out and then they make a monkey dance in the house!

Interaction Among Family Members

In a family, everyone learns to interact with people at all different stages of life. As a child grows up, he or she interacts with older people and with younger people— with grandparents, with parents, with brothers and sisters. That becomes the basis of a healthy psychological development. Otherwise, there is something lacking.

Interaction is extremely important for a perfect development of personality. If older people are rushed away from the family and put into old age homes, a child loses valuable interaction with them. There is a void created in families because of the absence of grandparents. That part of the education of children is missing in most families of the West.

As a result children are psychologically unable to handle the concept of aging and death, and this has many repercussions. So much so, that it makes them abnormal and perverted.

The presence of an old person in a family is to be viewed as an auspicious presence. No matter in which way a person may age, in a cultured society one must turn to the old person with respect. Sometimes old people will develop a strange nature, but despite that, the family should not be disrespectful towards them. Rather, they should always worship them. You must always turn to the feet of your grandmother no matter how senile she may be.

There are two blessings in a family: children and elders. No matter how childish your children are, you turn to them with affection; and similarly, no matter how "oldish" the older people become, you turn to them with adoration.

Those who have not practised *sadhana* (spiritual discipline) and are aging become uncontrolled. They cannot help it. But even that type of behavior is not completely out of place. Rather, it can give to a sensitive person growing in a family the message "Let me not become like that." Instead of hating, you become more sympathetic and realize that if you are not careful, you will become the same.

Education that comes through family is a sustaining education. You cannot get it in universities. A child receives one type of education from the mother, another from the father, another from an elderly person. All contribute to the building up of his personality. And if one or two persons in a family are not normal, even that helps the child realize what he must overcome in life.

Further, insight must develop that family relationship is based on *karma*. Souls have come together for a purpose. Though a particular interaction is apparently pleasant or painful, right or wrong, it has a spiritual significance. Sometimes great personalities come out of bitter families. Meera, for example, found herself in a family situation where she had nothing but bitterness from everyone—yet she became a great saint.

Thus, seen from a broader perspective, everything has its purpose. But this does not mean that you should condone lack of spirituality and disharmony in a family. Rather you should continue to promote harmony to the best of your capacity. If the family environment is not based on spiritual values, generally that family becomes a basis for creating weak-willed personalities.

Legal Freedom Versus Real Freedom

In Western culture, according to the law, a child is legally on their own at age twenty-one. Legally they can do whatever they want, without restriction from the parents. In India there is a family pressure that continues all through life, giving a protective hand to the children. Children should not look forward to that type of freedom in which they can do anything they want, without asking their parents. Rather, they should develop a friendship with their parents so that even when they become adults, the parents remain their friends.

Freedom from parents is not really any freedom at all—it will put a young person in the most miserable situation. The best freedom is when you have a friend, a guide in your father, your mother, your elders. Securing their blessings and love is very important. There must be an interaction between children and parents in which the parents are ready to sacrifice their old values when necessary and to adjust to the present demands, and the children will sacrifice the temptations that pressure their minds.

Arranged Marriages

In India, arranged marriages are based on dowries—and decisions are influenced by how much money the girl's father will give. That type of arrangement is absolutely wrong and is a bad tradition.

The dowry system as it has existed degrades the loving relationship, and educated people here should influence India to abolish it. The dowry should be an expression and token of love. Gifts should be given as symbols of a natural feeling—not as part of a business arrangement. Otherwise, anyone who is blessed with a baby daughter is not blessed—but rather cursed! As soon as the child is born, the father begins to think about how much money it will take to get her married. And that is highly degrading.

If Hindu parents of westernized children choose to follow the ancient tradition and insist on exercising their authority to arrange marriage, then the children will wait with great patience until legal age and then do what they want! If the arrangement of marriage is based only on an inflexible idea of the parents, then their authority will be worth nothing in the West. But if the arranged marriage is based upon the children's trust in their parents, it is far better.

In Hindu tradition, the emphasis is not given to love marriages, but to a marriage of mature judgement. Naturally, in the ideal Hindu set up, a young boy or girl growing in the West should seek the guidance of his parents, and it is through that guidance that the young person will know whom to choose as a mate.

As they grow up, your children should learn to think in a mature way and use their intellect. They should learn to make decisions along with you in a spirit of coopera- tion and friendship. They must feel that you understand them and try to help them. They must genuinely value your opinion.

It is a parent's great duty to earn the friendship, trust, and respect of his children. It causes much pain and distress in a family when there is no harmony or friendship. That friendship and harmony always re- quires some sacrifice, some adjustment, but the fruit of that sacrifice is very sweet and profound.

Cultural education has to be planted in the hearts of children so that they can choose their marriage partners for themselves in the right way, and they can remain friends with their parents as they grow up and begin their own families. If this does not happen, then there are going to be some negative results.

The Supreme Freedom

Along with a dynamic spiritual interdependence within the family, children should grow up with a sense of healthy freedom and independence. There is a great difference between Indian families and western families. Many westerners never had a family. To be separated from father, from mother, from brothers means nothing. But to an Indian mind it seems terrible to be separated. But that should not be so. If your family lives with a healthy philosophy, *vairagya* (dispassion) develops. You learn to see yourself as a spirit that is essentially free.

That development of *vairagya* does not mean that you become indifferent to the family. Rather you become more efficient in your life, more qualitative in your expressions, more harmonized in your dealings with others.

A sense of real freedom never causes hurt to others. Realization of the Self involves discovering an endless sense of freedom within you. And it will never hurt anyone. But, it is the lack of a sense of freedom that hurts everyone; no matter how good the situation may be. The supreme freedom lies in realizing God, and attaining liberation from the cycles of birth and death.

Mahatma Gandhi

5

WHAT IS LOVE?

Every
husband
should adore
the Devi or Goddess
who abides in his wife,
and every wife should worship
the God who abides in her husband.
This attitude of worship implies
a profound reverence for
the souls of each other.

With this attitude,
an ideal love evolves—
a love that sacrifices,
that waits with patience,
that is ever intent upon being
helpful and deeply compassionate.
Such a love is not thwarted by
adverse conditions of life;
rather, like the moon,
it shines brighter and
brighter as the
dark clouds of
adversity
pass on.

THE ILLUSION OF SEXUAL FREEDOM

There is a great misconception in today's world. Members of the modern generation feel that they are more culturally advanced than people who have come before them because they enjoy more freedom in the realm of senses than their forefathers enjoyed. They consider this so-called freedom as a mark of progress—as something highly desirable. But the truth is actually quite different.

Unbridled passion and uncontrolled sexuality existed in the past just as it does now. But in olden times it was considered negative by society. It was viewed as a taint of personality which an individual should not be proud of. An individual who was a prey to weaknesses was advised to seek the guidance of the wise. In the past, weaknesses in character were not adored nor sanctioned.

But today people have started worshipping their lower self. They are proud of sexual freedom. They are not ashamed of living a life of slavery to the senses. Young people in this materialistic society are led by the communications media and by the misguided example of many of their elders to believe that sex is fun and fun is what life is all about.

They are not aware of the fact that by their so-called sexual freedom they are degrading themselves physically, psychologically and morally, and in addition they are contributing to the degradation of society. Any promiscuity and frivolous sex-involvement leads to a debilitated mind, ill health, and a guilty conscience.

Any aspirant, regardless of age or stage of life, who is eager to attain Self-realization must not permit himself to be tempted by the lures of sex. If he submits to gross pleasures with the notion that later he will overcome them, he is terribly wrong. He becomes like a person who has placed his feet in quicksand—no matter how much he tries to free himself, he continues to sink deeper and deeper into illusions.

Thus, *grihasthis* (householders) and their children must deeply understand that in order to be truly successful, happy and fulfilled in life, they must reverence the human body and recognize the profound nature of the sex relationship. And ultimately, as they mature, their minds must eventually outgrow or outstep the illusion of sex altogether.

The mind that does not evolve beyond illusions of pleasure—and sex-pleasure is one of the most powerful illusions—carries those illusions into old age and even beyond! Thus you see many people who are in their seventies or eighties who are still imprisoned by those illusions. And the spirit moves from one body to another body, incarnation after incarnation, pursuing them.

A pleasure-loving person who runs from one mate to another until he is 90 years old is not really successful nor happy. He is in a most miserable situation. But once you begin to overcome that illusion, tremendous power is released within you and great virtuous qualities begin to unfold in your personality.

THE PATH TO
TRUE BRAHMACHARYA

Every religion speaks of the importance of overcoming lust and passion. However, the Hindu scriptures have given a profound insight into this process by detailing the mystic practice of *brahmacharya*.

"*Brahmacharya*" literally means living and moving in *Brahman*—the Absolute, and in its highest form, *brahmacharya* implies being established in the awareness, "I Am *Brahman*." However, from a relative point of view, *brahmacharya* is one of the *yamas* or restraints of Raja Yoga, and it is one of the most important foundations for one's spiritual movement. It consists of restraining the sex urge and sublimating it.

Physical Brahmacharya

According to the *Vedic* plan of life, one begins with *Brahmacharya Ashrama*—the stage of discipline and abstinence from sexual indulgence. As a student, your *Brahmacharya* was restricted to the body. That physical control of the sex urge—although only the beginning stage of true *brahmacharya*—is of great importance for success in every aspect of your life.

If, during your student life, you had developed
profound spiritual aspiration, you would have taken the
vow of *naishthika brahmachari* (a lifelong celibate). Some
great souls, due to their spiritual advancement in past
lives, attain a very high degree of physical and mental
purity even at an early age. When this is so, a *brahmachari*
student need not marry and enter *Grihastha Ashrama.* He
immediately embraces *sanyasa* or renunciation and strives
to experience Divine Love, wherein passion is totally
eradicated and sublimated.

On the other hand, if a student has practised *brahmacharya* physically, without gaining inner dispassion, then
the householder's stage provides the opportunity for
developing mental *brahmacharya*—the opportunity for
removing the roots of lust and passion from his unconscious mind.

In the householders stage, one develops fidelity
towards one's husband or wife. The sexual relationship
becomes a basis for channelizing one's sexual propensities. As higher love unfolds between husband and wife,
sexuality begins to diminish. Thus, a householder is
moving towards the attainment of *brahmacharya* in a
gradual manner.

Mental Brahmacharya

The practice of *brahmacharya* on this level demands
a vigilant watch over the mind. By self-introspection, one
must detect the presence of the sex thought immediately
as it arises and try to remove it by turning the mind to the
Divine Self. Whether one is a householder or a *sanyasi*,
whether one is married or a celibate, he must practise

mental *brahmacharya* by inward introspection and self-analysis. Mere external sex restraint is not enough.

If one does not strive to root out the subtle seeds of passion from his unconscious, then very often his suppressed lust will change into anger, and anger into greed. "Passion, anger and greed are triple gates to hell," says Sri Krishna in the *Gita*. These three are born of *rajas* (the distracted mode of mind) and exist as interrelated, interdependent sentiments. Though a person may develop the notion that he is practising *brahmacharya*, he will be deprived of the glorious powers of *brahmacharya* unless he has eradicated the seeds of all three of these vices through the profound understanding that he is not the body—he is essentially the Immortal Self.

Stepping Beyond Body-Consciousness

The need for sex, food and sleep is common to all living beings—animal as well as human. However, a human being possesses the special faculty of reflective intellect which distinguishes him from the majority of other living creatures on this earth. By purifying his intellect, he is able to control the sex urge and sublimate it into *ojas shakti* (spiritual force). By the power of his intuitive intellect he is able to transcend body consciousness itself.

According to the system of Kundalini Yoga, the *kundalini* (mystic energy) in the majority of people is confined to the three lower *chakras (Muladhara, Swadhishthana and Manipura)*. Therefore, their minds are ever immersed in thoughts of food, sex and various pleasures of the senses. But as one attains higher levels of evolution, the *kundalini* begins to operate through the higher *chakras (Anahata, Vishuddhi and Ajna Chakras)*, thereby revealing higher levels of consciousness.

For those who are immature, passion is mistaken for love. However, by cultivating purity of mind and intellect, an aspirant is able to overcome passion and convert it into pure love. Then the aspirant sees a clear contrast between the fleeting and deceptive pleasures of the senses and the pure joys of the Self revealed through the purified states of mind. As one thus overcomes the dependence upon the senses for experiencing happiness, he is able to seek higher forms of happiness and inner fulfillment through the planes of the higher Self within.

Preoccupation with sex has its roots in body identification (identifying yourself as a male or female). However, in reality, the innermost spirit in a person is neither male nor female, and is unaffected by the characteristics of the physical body. Led by different *karmas*, an individual soul may incarnate as a male in one birth and as a female in another. Once you deeply understand that you are spirit, you are no longer enslaved by gender and, even in your lifetime, you overcome sex consciousness as well as body identification itself.

When human beings see each other as bodies, they are putting each other in a degraded position. But when they see each other as spirit, it is very uplifting. The body may appear to be the most important thing about another person in the beginning of a relationship, but as your intellect matures you realize that the body is just a cloth. The spirit is beyond body, beyond sexes.

Brahmacharya for Householders

As you can well see, entering into *Grihastha Ashrama* does not imply that there is no more need of *brahmacharya*. On the contrary, for the wise householder who aspires for the highest in life, marriage is just another step toward the subtler practise of *brahmacharya*. The very purpose of married life is to give meaning and direction to sexual propensities, so that deeper forms of love may be gradually realized. In the course of time, in a truly successful marriage, there need be no dependence on sexuality between husband and wife. They become more internally communicative—profound friends who help each other for the attainment of the fourfold purposes of life: ethical, material, social and spiritual.

Only in such a mature love can the insecurity that plagues most couples vanish. If pleasure is the only bond in a marriage, no one knows who will be divorced first! But when sexuality is no longer considered the essence of your relationship, you do not have to be afraid of aging and becoming physically unattractive to your husband or wife. You do not have to fear being deserted if illness or injury impairs your beauty or strength. Your relationship blossoms into the union of two spirits—rather than two bodies.

Keeping this in view, fidelity in marriage becomes of paramount importance. And even within the bond of marriage, a couple should develop a healthy restraint and self-control. Married life should become a means to understanding, removing and sublimating the subtle propensities of sexuality that abide in the unconscious, and should pave the way for the unfoldment of Divine Love in the stages of *vanaprastha* (asceticism) and *sanyasa* (renunciation). In these last two stages, the tree of *brahmacharya*—which developed its first shoots during student life, and sent out luxuriant branches during householder life—flourishes with the blossoms of Divine qualities and the nectarine fruit of Self-realization.

The Evolution of Love

Thus *Grihastha Ashram* was not meant to contradict *brahmacharya*, but was meant to perfect *brahmacharya*. You start to cultivate *brahmacharya* in *Brahmacharya Ashram*. Then you are led to greater perfection in *brahmacharya* through *Grihastha Ashram*. And then, as you enter *Vanaprastha*, you learn more about how to meditate on *Brahman*, how to abide in *Brahman*. In *Sanyasa* stage, when you attain enlightenment, you are a full *brahmachari*. You live and move in *Brahman*—which is the real meaning of *brahmacharya*.

To see how beautifully the plan operates, imagine that you had a tender shoot of a Banyan tree that you hoped one day would grow to be a mighty tree and express its great Banyan nature. You fence it in so that the goat will not come and eat it up, and when you see the goat trying to enter, you drive it away. If the young plant had the power to speak it might say, "Why are you doing all this to me? Why are you putting fences around me. Let me be." Well, you know that the plant might not survive unharmed if you listened to its complaint, so you continue to protect it with your wisdom and experience.

Similarly, young people in their tender student days are introduced to the concept of *brahmacharya* with little restraints of the mind and senses. If your teenage son or daughter were to say, "Why should you control me? Why do you discipline me? Let me be!"—your heart must answer, "I do so so that one day you can express all the inner majesty and potentiality that is your birthright."

Fencing in is an important aspect in student life so that the mind is not scattered through distraction. When you enter *grihastha* life, you have grown a great deal, but still you are not a stout, full-grown spiritual aspirant. You still need guidance and protection. As a *vanaprasthi* and then an enlightened *sanyasi*, you finally become gigantic and fully rooted in the indestructible Spirit. When you become one with *Brahman* you have attained absolute perfection in *brahmacharya*.

The Power of Brahmacharya

Sri Ramakrishna Paramahamsa was of the view that if one practised *brahmacharya* successfully for seven years, all the *chakras* of *kundalini* would be awakened effortlessly. Many great sages and saints have given similar views. Yogic scriptures point out that sex-energy, *prana* and mind are intimately related. By controlling sex-energy, one harmonizes the *pranas* and promotes meditative states of the mind. The *Raja Yoga Sutras* of Patanjali Maharshi state that one who is established in *brahmacharya* attains an abundance of physical , mental and spiritual energy. *Brahmacharya* tones the nerves, nourishes the brain, harmonizes the *pranas*, and elevates the mind. It is the foundation of all Divine qualities.

Mahatma Gandhi was of the view that *brahmacharya* must be practised by all those who wish to serve humanity in an effective way—because *brahmacharya* endows a person with special spiritual strength. Mahatma Gandhi was a great exponent of nonviolence, truthfulness and *brahmacharya*, the three most important *yamas* (ethical restraints). He emphasized the fact that if these virtues were taught, culture would rise to a very high level and manifold problems of humanity would be effectively solved. On the other hand, if these ideals are not impressed on the minds of people, human culture would be terribly degraded and would be led to disaster.

Today's youth are constantly exposed to the charms of materialistic culture through films, TV shows, and radio programs. It is for this reason that the ideal of *brahmacharya* seems like such an impossibility for most people. However, if these media of communication were to present examples of great men who mastered their mind and senses, and who practised lives of purity—Jesus Christ, Buddha, Shankaracharya, Mahatma Gandhi, Ramana Maharshi, Ramakrishna Paramahamsa, and other sages and saints who have inspired mankind—the minds of our youth would be drawn to the lofty goals of spiritual life. What great treasure lies in the human heart! By controlling passion, one can enjoy the indescribable sweetness of Divine Love and become immersed in God.

6

YOGA IN LIFE

Let there be harmony
between husband and wife.
Let there be harmony
between parents and their children.
Let there be harmony
among different relatives.
Let there be harmony among friends.
Let there be harmony among nations.
Let there be harmony among the elements.
Let there be harmony
between the earth and the sky.
Let harmony be experienced
everywhere!

HARMONIZE YOUR LIFE

Those who study the *Upanishads* and other Yogic scriptures are often confused because there are seemingly two types of teachings in the scriptures: teachings that extol the need of *sanyasa* or renunciation, and teachings that glorify selfless action. An aspirant wonders, "Should I renounce my job and family and go to the Himalayas, or should I remain as a *grihasthi* or householder?"

Similar confusions plague spiritual seekers of every religion. When Christians read the injunction of Lord Jesus "Seek ye first the kingdom of Heaven" they wonder, "But how am I supposed to do this?" Many say, "I'll seek the Kingdom of Heaven when I get older—when I won't have anything else to do. What's the rush now? The kingdom I'm living in right now looks fine to me."

An aspirant must understand the important fact that spiritual movement is an enrichment of one's life. To grasp this more fully, imagine that there is a tree in a forest that wishes to express itself more fully and become more beautiful. One day the breeze brings it a message: "Bedeck yourself with flowers and make yourself colorful." Then right after this the tree gets another message: "Don't do that at all; it's nonsense. What you must do instead is to try to send your roots as deep into the ground as possible." The two suggestions seem contradictory, and the tree is confused. "Should I attend to my roots, or should I concentrate on blossoming?"

The fact is that both alternatives are two aspects of the same process. Finding one's roots, however, is the more important; it is toward your roots that you must direct your self-effort. If the tree were to send its roots deep into the earth and find a virtually boundless reservoir of water and nutrients, it would then enjoy great health and beauty.

Similarly, if a person were to find his roots in God, the Divine Self, everything about him—including his personality, his relationships, his business affairs, his role in society—would be transformed and he would be truly prosperous and successful.

Furthermore, when a tree blossoms it not only becomes beautiful, but fragrant as well; indeed, its fragrance drifts beyond the tree and permeates the entire atmosphere. Similarly, when you enrich yourself through spiritual attainment, your personality wafts a fragrance that is heavenly, and your contribution to the world becomes unimaginably great. A person who has attained heights of spirituality, or higher levels of integration, becomes a center, as it were, radiating peace, harmony, goodwill, and positive thoughts. All these emanate from him like the fragrance of a thousand flowers.

In order for you to send your roots deep into the bedrock of wisdom, three things are most important: you need to have a profound insight into what liberation is, you need to make it your goal, and you need to practise the techniques that lead you to the goal with great patience and perseverance.

You gain insight or knowledge by studying the scriptures through the medium of *satsanga*, or positive association with the wise. When you study the great scriptures with patience and under proper guidance you realize that the goal of cosmic consciousness is not far away; it is deep within your own heart. The fact is that you are essentially Divine. Every religion declares that in its own special way. In the *Vedantic* tradition, however, this is spoken of with particularly great fervor—*"Tat Twam Asi"*—"Thou Art That!"

Does not the *Bible* say, "I and the Father are one," "The Kingdom of Heaven is within you," "Know ye not that ye are Gods?" Everywhere the scriptures are telling you that you are essentially Divine; you are not the personality that you think you are. In fact, you are already rooted in God. It is just a matter of discovering this truth. Without God how can a person exist? Human life has never really been in the hands of the ego! How could ego guide all the intricate mechanisms of your body? How could ego control even a single cell?

When you begin to reflect on the things that you hear through *satsanga* you realize that your deeper roots have always been in God. Without God you cannot exist.

God is not something or somebody completely apart from you, existing somewhere in the vastness of the universe. God is your innermost essence. The *Upanishads* have presented this teaching in the form of questions: Who is the mind of the mind, the eye of the eye? Who is the knower, who is the seer? As you begin to understand and develop these insights you realize that to find God you do not have to go anywhere; all that is involved in finding Him is changing the pattern of your mind. The *Upanishads* declare: *"Mana eva manushyaanam, kaaranam bandha mokshayoh"*—"Mind is the cause of bondage and release."

When you still the mind and free it of the burden of unconscious complexes you get an immediate revelation that you are not the ego; you are not this perishable personality. You are one with God, the Divine Self. And because of this nothing can shake you.

In *Yoga Vasistha* it is written that even if there were a great catastrophe and the whole earth were to explode, causing burning embers to rain down everywhere, you would remain unshaken if you had the experience of being rooted in God. This poetic imagery shows the feeling of invincibility that can be awakened in an individual when he realizes that his roots are in God—and have always been in God.

Integrating your Life in a Harmonious Way

The *Bhagavad Gita*, which is one of the most important scriptures of Yoga, outlines four great paths to the revelation of truth: action, meditation, devotion, and wisdom. Blending these four harmoniously in daily life gives one the best technique for attaining Self-realization.

The Path of Action

The path of action is referred to as *Karma Yoga* in Yoga philosophy. It implies that you develop an attitude of worshiping God through the duties that you have to perform. There are two kinds of duties, broadly speaking: those arising out of your family situation or your job—i.e., your personal responsibilities in daily life— and those related to your eagerness to serve humanity.

At a very advanced stage everything you do can be thought of as service to God. But until that spirit develops you need to promote selflessness, and let your actions reach out beyond the needs of your own personality or that of your relatives. You should always have a project that will help other people. Ask yourself what it is that you can do best for other people. Marshal the special talents that God has endowed you with and serve others.

Of course the *Vedic* tradition offers a wonderful outlet for doing this by encouraging aspirants to spend time in an *ashram* and to serve its spiritual mission. By helping to publish spiritual literature and by bringing knowledge to others in various ways, you are actually helping humanity most effectively. The best help that one can render to other people is to spread spiritual knowledge that helps others aspire for and attain enlightenment.

Apart from that, performing any selfless action of any kind can be thought of as *Karma Yoga*. Whatever duties that your nature inclines you toward should not be personalized. By this I mean that the actions you perform should get you out of yourself; they should encourage you to feel that you are dedicating your energy and talent to improving society at large. And while working selflessly, whether for your family, society, or yourself, you sacrifice your labor to God. According to the *Gita*, even the act of eating is a sacrifice—a form of worship of God. The spirit that proclaims that every action is a form of worship is *Karma Yoga*. When that spirit develops your mind does not center itself on the fruit of action.

People nowadays are much more interested in the fruit of their labor than in the merits of their labor; accomplishing the task is all that matters. Under pressure to get the job done "by hook or by crook," we have taken to leaning and depending on technology more and more. This form of erroneous vision is the basis of much of the stress that has developed in society. Pressure to accomplish tasks faster and faster has made life much more tense.

A spiritual aspirant should cultivate the art of enjoying the work he is doing instead of just doing it to get the job done. The very process of performing a task should be enjoyable. The essence of *Karma Yoga* lies in the insight that by performing your duties without leaning upon the fruits of action, you are promoting *chitta-shuddhi*, or purity of the heart.

Once this understanding develops you remain balanced whether your projects succeed or not. You are satisfied that the work you have accomplished has given you some internal fulfillment which no one can take away from you. Even when you do not succeed at a project you acquire willpower and an inner satisfaction that you have done your duty. Thus, it is so important to cultivate the spirit of *Karma Yoga* in your daily life.

The Path of Meditation

The next important aspect of Yoga that must be harmoniously blended in your daily life is meditation. Learn the art of meditation and practise it every day. The best time to meditate is early in the morning from four to six o'clock. This time period is known as *Brahmamuhurta*.

Start by setting aside half an hour for your practice. When you are relaxed and ready to concentrate, light a candle and some incense, and then fix your gaze on a Deity or whatever ideal you wish to meditate upon. Then sit comfortably and let your mind flow peacefully towards the object of meditation. Follow this process of meditation and try to still your mind day-by-day. Regular meditation will help you think more clearly, comprehend life's subtler points, and also give you more concentration for the work at hand. When you work at a task with a dissipated mind it takes a long time to accomplish it; but with a concentrated mind you can accomplish a great deal of work and remain relaxed.

Meditation thus becomes a gateway to great achievements. As you practise meditation, you explore the heights that mind can achieve. Super-consciousness, intuitional experiences, profound insights—all these await one who follows the path of meditation.

The Path of Devotion

The next aspect of Yoga to be blended in your life is devotion, or love of God. Most of the world's religions emphasize this path. If one has love of God it makes the path to liberation easier, because it helps to efface one's ego. Ego is a great obstacle to spiritual advancement, and devotion dissolves it faster than any other method.

Day by day one should develop the clear understanding that God is the source of infinite love. Your soul has been seeking that love, trying to discover it through many embodiments. That inner urge is there in every individual to find someone or something that can be loved with tremendous and intense fulfillment. But this urge leads one into many *karmic* entanglements. You try to find love through husbands, wives, and children. But when the *karma* for such relative love is over, you can no longer find the perfect love you envisioned in those associations. The scene then changes and you soon have a whole different set of people around you.

Ultimately, when your mind turns to God you realize that it is actually He who makes people shine with life and beauty. When you find delight in friends, that delight actually comes because God is in them. Once God withdraws His glory from a person's body it lies dead, all its beauty fading in a single moment.

Japa, or repetition of *mantra*, is a very simple yet effective means for developing devotion for God. Train your mind to repeat any Divine name again and again, as if it were psychic sugar candy. Try to think of nothing else as you do this. Repeating a mystic formula daily does a great deal to build up impressions of spiritual strength in your unconscious.

Prayer is another important means of coming closer to God. When you pray you open your heart to God, no matter what form of prayer you adopt. To guide you in developing the art of prayer, read devotional literature. In all the religions of the world there are examples and stories from the lives of sages and saints that illustrate the power of prayer. Read the prayers they recited during trying times in their lives. Try to develop the love of God that was the crowning glory of their lives.

The Path of Knowledge

Finally we come to the path of knowledge. This entails a thorough, day by day study of the scriptures, such as the *Gita, Yoga Vasistha, Upanishads,* or any other works that give you philosophical insight. Studying these scriptures exercises your reason, and you will be led to understand that the real You is neither the body nor the mind. You are essentially the Absolute Self!

When you are ignorant of this fact, you are as if hypnotized. Each day you impress upon yourself that you are this body, that your happiness depends upon objects, and that if only you could accomplish a certain thing you would be happy. Even when you turn towards spirituality you still hypnotize yourself by saying, "I am so far away from the spiritual goal; it may take me a hundred births to attain it." By judging yourself like this you are putting an obstacle in your path. On the other hand, instead of allowing your mind to move in this negative direction, again and again try to relax your mind and reflect upon your true nature: you are essentially the Divine Self!

The Path of "Littles" Will Lead You Home

If you practise these four points everyday, even in small measure, you will make significant progress on the road to liberation. To be spiritual you do not have to do something totally fantastic like walk the length of the United States, wade into the cold waters of the Ganges River at three o'clock in the morning, or fast for forty days. The notion that you have to do something bizarre and uncomfortable to be a spiritual person is entirely wrong.

Actually you do greater austerity when you harmonize yourself day by day. The person who meditates a little, reflects a little, does some devotional practices, and surrenders himself to God while doing his daily chores is going to make much greater progress than the person who subjects his body to dramatic austerities.

Of course, a spiritual aspirant should understand that there are going to be ups and downs in his daily practice of *sadhana*; human life does not unfold in a straight line. Problems often make one take backward steps. In spite of these changing circumstances, try to balance yourself to whatever extent you can as you practise the four paths of Yoga. Daily, sustained effort on the spiritual path is far more important than the greatest austerities you can imagine. Harmony of spiritual practice is much more effective than the most glaring kinds of austerity and work, for it is actually a more intensive kind of spiritual movement. Furthermore, if you do practise spiritual discipline harmoniously, nothing will ever change abruptly in your life; rather, your life will become increasingly enriched.

Think of the tree that I talked about earlier. The moment it sends its roots deep into the earth and draws the richness from it, it begins to flourish. Similarly, the moment you seek your roots in God through harmonization of yourself, your personality flourishes; you bring the best you have to all your relationships with others. You become a shining example to society at large, and everyone around you becomes inspired. You will be astounded at how easily all this can happen if you harmonize your life. That is the secret.

Thus, resolve to practise a blend of dedicated action, devotion, meditation and reflection in daily life, and always keep the goal before you—the goal of Self-realization. May God bless you with harmony and peace!

THE SPIRITUAL VALUE
OF CONFLICT

Conflict abounds everywhere in human life. There are conflicts among various religions, each asserting that their system is the only way to God and criticizing all others. There are conflicts among various philosophers and philosophical views, each upholding his own system as the best and criticizing others. There are conflicts in human relationships and in society. You expect to have sunshine, but God arranges to have dark clouds in the sky. Conflicts of different types arise at every step of life. Conflict is everywhere.

Often an aspirant develops the idea that if life were without conflict, things would be wonderful—an idea that, in itself, creates conflict in the mind. Deluded by that faulty understanding, many aspirants go on looking for a perfect situation where conflicts do not exist. Some even look for that type of setup in some remote place high in the Himalayas. And many adopt different types of spiritual systems—some becoming ascetics, observing fasts or undergoing severe disciplines of the senses, or observing *mouna* or silence for a long time.

But if you were to objectively reflect upon the value of conflict, you would realize that there would be no spiritual progress if there were no conflict. Conditions of conflict provide resistance, and resistance is needed for a strong movement. If a person were given all favorable conditions in life, he would become like a jellyfish, having no muscles, no strength, and a cramped spiritual movement.

At times your views are criticized. Not only are you criticized verbally, but also subjected to physical misery. You must not despair. You should not think that these situations of conflict have nothing but negative value for you and that you would have been much better off without them. Reflect upon the examples of great men— history is replete with such examples. Jesus was not only criticized but subjected to crucifixion, and yet he accepted all this with a spirit of resignation to the Divine Will. Socrates was given poison, and he accepted it with a poised mind. These are just a few examples of how great men continue to tread the path of righteousness unaffected by conditions of conflict. Rather, in their case, these conditions prove to be blessings in disguise.

It is important to understand that you cannot live your life without conflicts. If you take a bucket of water out of a quiet lake, the surrounding water immediately rushes in to fill the empty spot. The water around that area becomes in conflict and rushes in to fill the hole. Similarly, the moment there is an area of low pressure in the atmosphere, the surrounding atmosphere pushes into that low pressure region and the winds begin to blow. In the same way, nature will not allow anyone to rest in the world of time and space. Conflicts are the "Hounds of Heaven" that will follow the heels of your soul until you attain the state of liberation, in which the world of time and space is transcended.

Conflicts are needed in the Divine Plan. Behind what appears as agitating, tumultuous and confusing, there is a Divine Plan—a plan to promote peace and harmony.

An aspirant, however, should not himself create conflicting situations. When you see people in harmony, do not just walk up to them and start disturbing them. But when conflicting conditions arise by themselves, an aspirant must be able to just sit back and not become involved or affected; he should learn to just wait and watch. And in spite of those conditions, he must continue his spiritual effort. Sometimes it may seem that he cannot do as much *sadhana* or spiritual practice as he would have if there were no disturbing conditions, but the fact is that whatever little *sadhana* he does in the midst of conflict has a greater value than *sadhana* performed at other times.

For example, when you are doing mechanical work such as putting some shelves together, and you have to hammer a nail into a certain area, it is not how much you hammer or how much strength you use that counts, but where you hammer. And if you hammer in the right place, then just a little hammering is enough to do the job. In the same manner, it is not how much *sadhana* you practise that is important—how many hours you meditate, how long you practice *japa*—but the intensity, sincerity and quality with which you practice it. So even in adverse situations, whatever *sadhana* you are able to do has great value.

On the other hand, if you do not know the art of handling conflict, you will develop an escapist philosophy. The moment there is a situation that your ego does not like, you will run away from it, promoting a weak personality. However, no matter where you run, there will always be something lacking within yourself. There will always be something that will create new conflicts. In the course of time, situations of frustration will develop again.

So, therefore, aspirants must learn the art of adapting and adjusting, and of not becoming frustrated by conflict. Rather, they must understand that no matter where they go, if they are to evolve, God will present challenging situations. Such situations are designed to cultivate willpower, to test faith, and to bring out what is good within.

As aspirant's movement is much like winnowing grain. When farmers collect grain, the technique adopted in separating the husk from the grain is to pour the grain from one container into another. As the wind passes through the grain, the husk is blown away, leaving the grain pure. In the same manner, conditions of conflict are like the blowing winds. If you are pursuing the spiritual path with faith and patience, all the husks of sickness, weakness and unwanted things in your life will be blown away, while all that is of value and importance will settle down within your heart.

That is the purpose of conflict, and the same applies to society and, from a broader point of view, to the world. When there are clashes in ideologies, clashes in different political situations, and clashes of various types, people seem to live a life of turmoil. But notice how all these conflicting situations pass on and things of greater value eventually dominate the minds of people. Therefore, there is a purpose behind conflicting situations in the world, in your life, and in your relationships. Out of conflicting thoughts and beliefs, there emerges the desired environment conducive to harmony and peace.

As you develop insight into the philosophy of conflict, you understand that conflicting situations are giving you a test—a test to your faith and understanding. Then you understand that these situations are providing a better opportunity for your spiritual evolution. With this insight you begin to smile at conflicts and you develop that type of mind which is not upset by conflict. The idea that somewhere and someday you will find the most ideal situation will fade away from your mind. Rather, you will realize that here and now you have the best circumstances, the most ideal conditions.

Once your mind settles upon this type of understanding, you have gained a firm foothold on the path of spiritual movement. Your movement will then be steady and definite. You are bound to succeed. But as long as there is an internal conflict or sense of dissatisfaction with the way things are, or the idea that somewhere else in the distant future you will find a better situation, then you cannot take advantage of all that is given to you by nature. Therefore, try to reflect upon the value of conflict and develop a mind that confronts conflict with a smile and spiritual vision.

Lord Shiva

7

UPASANA
OR MEDITATION

Upasana
purifies your heart,
destroys negative karmas,
creates positive impressions
in the unconscious,
wards off obstacles in life,
and endows you with
countless blessings
as it creates a
profound change
in your personality.

MEDITATION ON OM

The highest form of *upasana* is *nirguna nirakara upasana*—or meditation on *Brahman* without attributes or form. In order to facilitate meditation upon *Brahman* in this manner, *Om* has been designated in the *Upanishads* as the most perfect symbol of *Brahman*.

In this stage of advanced meditation on *Om*, *upasana* (devout meditation) and *vichar* (enquiry) actually blend. *Upasana* is the process of meditation in which one adopts one's own attitude; *vichar* is the process in which one sacrifices one's attitude to recognize the truth as it is—it is the process of enquiry and reflection. Although these two processes are distinct, they blend in this advanced practice of *Om Upasana*. One has to be deeply reflective in order to promote this meditation.

Om has four aspects which can be represented by the letters A, U, M and the *ardha-matra* (which is silent according to Sanskrit grammar). An aspirant practises this meditation by relaxing his body and mind with the mental repetition of *Om* and, along with this, he reflects upon the implications and subtle meaning of each of the aspects of A-U-M-*ardha-matra*.

Meditation on the "A" Aspect

The "A" aspect of *Om* refers to the physical body, the physical plane, and waking consciousness. It also represents *Virat*, the Cosmic Being, which includes all physical bodies.

As you repeat *Om*, try to feel that you are the physical body. You won't have much difficulty doing this because you identify yourself with your body every day. But what is the physical body?

The physical body is formed out of the five elements drawn from the cosmos. At every moment of your life, your cells are disintegrating and diffusing back into the cosmos. Thus, you draw from the cosmos and diffuse back into it. Since you are inseparably related to the cosmos, you should understand and affirm, "If I am the physical body, I am also the universal body."

Just as a wave is related to the ocean, so too is the physical body related to the entire physical universe. "If I am the physical body, then I am also the ocean, the earth, the moon, the planets, the sun, the stars—I am all." From a very simple observation, you bring your mind to an elevated understanding. All of this is quite reasonable. It isn't some vain type of imagining. However, great imagination and insight is involved in extending one's understanding to include the idea that the entire universe is oneself.

As you dwell on the "A" aspect, you can also reflect upon the waking state and attempt to understand what it implies. When you are awake, you think of yourself as being a particular person living in a certain country, belonging to a certain race. Naturally you have certain

realities because your body is a product of *karma*. When
that *karmic* process terminates, you will leave your present body and enter another one.

So, viewed from a broader perspective, your waking
state becomes like a dream. You move from one body to
another. The waking state is a transient state; it is not
intrinsic. As this reflection matures, you develop insight
that you are beyond the physical body. You are the subtle
body. Then your mind focuses itself on the "U" aspect of
Om.

Meditation on the "U" Aspect

The "U" aspect of *Om* refers to the dream state, the
astral body, and the cosmic totality of all astral bodies
known as *Hiranyagarbha* or the cosmic mind. At this
stage, you focus your attention first on the understanding that you are the astral or subtle body. Your physical
body is just a tool. Your deeper personality is subtle. It is
composed of vital forces, mind, senses, and intellect. And
again, from a deeper point of view, you understand that
your subtle body is not an individualized entity; it is a
wave in the cosmic subtle body which is *Hiranyagarbha*,
the cosmic mind. Thus you are linked to the cosmic
mind. Your thoughts do not originate in the ego-self;
they proceed from the cosmic mind. As your ego relaxes,
your mind becomes a channel for cosmic thoughts.

Thus, try to understand the possibility of uniting
your mind with the cosmic mind. Try to understand that
the Divine mind permeates your mind; the Divine subtle
body permeates your individual subtle body. This form
of reflection and devout meditation along with mental

repetition of *Om* comprises the "U" aspect of meditation on *Om*.

Meditation on the "M" Aspect

Finally, you focus your attention on the "M" aspect of *Om*. The "M" aspect of *Om* refers to the causal body, which is beyond mind and intellect. This is the vast realm of the unconscious. During deep sleep you are identified with your causal body. The causal body itself is a highly advanced center within you. Nevertheless, during sleep you do not have a positive experience of the causal body. That is why all that you experience in deep sleep is the absence of duality, absence of the awareness of time and space.

So, the "M" aspect of *Om* represents the causal body. Your causal body is related to the cosmic causal body, which in Sanskrit is called *Ishwara* or God. God is the cosmic source of all. An individual causal body is linked to God just as a wave is linked to the ocean. Thus, at the "M" stage, you try to understand that the deeper core of your existence is one with God.

Meditation on the Ardha-Matra Aspect

Finally we come to the fourth aspect of *Om*—the *ardha-matra*, which is silence. When *Om* is uttered, it is followed by a brief pause of silence. This is represented by a *vindu* or point. It refers to the transcendental state beyond waking, dream, and deep sleep. In this aspect of the meditation, one affirms, "I am beyond the body, mind, senses, intellect, ego—even beyond the causal body. I am one with *Brahman*."

Thus, along with mental chanting of *Om*, there is constant affirmation and constant reflection upon one's higher nature. In the reflective process, you are constantly detaching yourself from the body, senses, mind, intellect, ego and from the vast realm of the unconscious. You detach yourself from all these and assert that you are *Brahman*, the Absolute Self.

This, in brief, is the nature of *Pranava Upasana* or *Om Upasana*. *Om* is called *pranava*, which literally means "ever new." In the beginning of your practice of this meditation, you may think that you have understood all about it and have reached all the boundaries of reflection on *Om*. But as you advance, you realize that the boundaries of *Om* are limitless. Even the implications of the very first letter "A" are so profound that you will be amazed as you continue to practise.

Om As the Basis of Saguna Upasana

Most of the *mantras* (Divine names) begin with *Om*—such as *Om Sri Ramaya Namah, Om Namah Sivaya, Om Sri Krishnaya Namah, Om Namo Narayanaya, Om Sri Mahalakshmyai Namah*, and so forth.

While chanting *Om* mentally, you may meditate upon your *Ishta Devata* (the chosen Deity such as Vishnu, Shiva, or Devi). Think of the Divine attributes of peace, bliss, compassion, infinity, beauty, knowledge, power and so forth.

Even the verbal chanting of *Om* creates a soothing effect on one's body; it harmonizes the *pranas* (the vital forces), and strengthens one's nervous system.

You may choose simply *Om* as your *mantra*, and as you repeat *Om*, feel the presence of the Divine Self enveloping you. *Om* encompasses the two limits of the field of human speech. With "A" you open your mouth, with "M" you close your lips. When you have said *Om* (A+U+M) you have used the entire vocal range from the throat to the lips, thus symbolizing the fact that you have uttered all that is to be uttered. Therefore, the sages chose *Om* as the verbal symbol of the all-encompassing God or *Brahman*.

MEDITATION
ON GAYATRI MANTRA

Gayatri Upasana is meditation on the Divine Self using a special *mantra* taken from the *Vedas*. It is considered the "mother of *mantras*" and is an extension of *Om* or *Pranava Upasana.* As you recall, *Om* is the symbol of the Absolute Self, and meditation on that Self is further intensified with the help of repetition of *Gayatri Mantra.*

Gayatri Mantra was composed by illumined sages for the purpose of leading spiritual aspirants to the glorious summits of spiritual evolution and final liberation. Composed originally in a metrical style known as *"gayatri,"* the *mantra* came to be called *Gayatri Mantra* as it became increasingly popular. In a deeper sense, the word *"gayatri"* implies "that which leads one to liberation," or "that which protects one from fear of the world process."

Since *Gayatri Mantra* is a *mantra* glorifying the Divine Self, you may repeat this *mantra* in addition to your *Ishta mantra.* It will supplement your *Ishta mantra.* On the other hand, you may choose *Gayatri Mantra* as your *Ishta mantra,* or you may chose this *mantra* as a basis for your meditation.

Here is the *Gayatri Mantra* and its literal meaning:

ॐभूर्भुवः स्वः
तत् सवितुर् वरेण्यम्
भर्गो देवस्य धीमहि
धियो यो नः प्रचोदयात् ॥

Om bhoor bhuvah swah
Tat savitur varenyam
Bhargo devasya dheemahi
Dhiyo yo nah prachodayat.

"*Om*" refers to *Brahman,* the Divine Self. "*Bhoor bhuvah swah*" refer to the physical, astral, and causal planes, which are popularly referred to as the three worlds. According to the sages, the universe consists of three planes: *bhoor* is the physical plane, *bhuvah* is the astral, and *swah* is the causal.

"*Tat*" means "That," "*savitur*" is "sun," "*varenyam*" means "adorable one."

"*Bhargo*" means "effulgence or luminosity," "*devasya*" means "of that God," "*dheemahi*" means " we adore."

"*Dhiyo*" refers to intellect, "*yo nah*" means "our," and "*prachodayat*" means "may He illumine."

Thus, taken in its entirety, *Gayatri Mantra* literally means: "*Om.* We adore that *Brahman,* the Supreme Self, who, like the sun, illumines the three planes of existence, the entire universe. May He illumine our intellect—for the attainment of Self-realization."

When this *mantra* is repeated it renders the intellect subtle, pure and bright. It also enhances willpower. Because of this, repetition of the *Gayatri Mantra* is especially enjoined for *brahmacharis* (those who are students) in Hindu culture. This *mantra* may be recited in the morning, at noon, and in the evening. However, you may repeat this powerful *mantra* any time you wish and enjoy its effectiveness.

Devotees desirous of liberation, aspirants striving for self-control and conservation of energy, students eager to develop memory power and the ability to comprehend the subtle meaning of the *Vedas*, and all those desiring a favorable development in life have been repeating the *Gayatri Mantra* and invoking Divine Grace through it for thousands of years in India. The *mantra* has thus gathered a unique spiritual association.

Constant mental repetition of *Gayatri mantra*, coupled with meditation on the Light of the Self and with a sincere prayer for enlightenment, brings brilliance to one's personality and enhances the magnetic power or spiritual force *(ojas shakti)* of whomever repeats it.

Gayatri Mantra removes various impediments and destroys negative *karmas*. Its benefits have been eloquently described in the *Vedas*. Indeed, there are immense benefits to be had through repetition of the *Gayatri Mantra*, but you should not expect to have them all immediately because there are many factors that delay the expression of these benefits.

A story is told of a saintly person who repeated this *mantra* thousands of times, yet never had a vision of the deity. As a result, he became frustrated. He said to himself, "Why should I repeat my *mantra*? It has done nothing for me." During the night he had a dream in which he saw seventeen great piles of wood burning. The deity told him, "These piles of wood represent your negative *karmas*. Since you did seventeen *purashcharanas* (repetition of a *mantra* for so many thousands of times) of your *mantra*, seventeen big heaps of negative *karmas* have been burned up. And because it took all this time for your negative *karmas* to be consumed by the fire, you didn't see any tangible results from your repeating the *mantra*; nevertheless, your *mantra* was in constant operation." All aspirants must understand this lesson well and realize that repetition of *mantra* is a subtle but infallible process of inner transformation.

In repeating the *Gayatri Mantra* you ask for enlightenment and nothing else—and for good reason: there is no prayer greater than asking for enlightenment. Once your intellect is illumined, you need nothing else—for you discover that you are the Self—Existence, Knowledge, and Bliss Absolute!

Meditation on Gayatri Mantra

During the practice of meditation, an aspirant should repeat this *mantra* mentally. The mantra has four parts. While repeating each part, a specific mental attitude should be maintained.

The first part—*Om bhoor bhuvah swah*—refers to expansion. Therefore, as you repeat the Sanskrit words mentally, meditate upon the infinite expansion that embraces the three planes of existence, the entire universe.

While repeating *Tat savitur varenyam*, meditate upon Absolute Consciousness, the Light of all lights, which permeates the entire universe. God is like the effulgent sun which permeates the three worlds. Divine glory is inherent in every object of the world and is resplendent glory—glory which is not hidden. It is hidden from your view only due to ignorance. If you were enlightened you would see that the whole world is the radiation from the Divine Self; it is the scintillating light of God.

As you repeat *Bhargo devasya dheemahi*, meditate upon the Light of the Self shining upon the summits of your intellect. Feel that you are invoking the Divine Presence in your heart and that you are being filled with Divine Consciousness. The rays of the sun turn the snows of the mountains into dazzling gold. In the same way pray that wisdom may rise and shine within you, and that your intellect may receive its light and shine like gold.

While repeating *Dhiyo yo nah prachodayat*, develop a sense of supreme surrender of the ego and the perception of the transcendental Self.

Thus, in four stages, you are meditating upon infinite existence or limitless expansion, the Light of spiritual consciousness, invocation of the spiritual Light in your being, and the experience of enlightenment.

In brief, here is the formula to be associated with *Gayatri Mantra*: expansion, illumination, surrender, and Divine communion or Realization.

As you practise this meditation, recite the *mantra* mentally with a relaxed but serene mind. You may wish to adopt physical or concrete symbols to lead your mind into the depths of meditation.

For example, mentally visualize the rising sun. Think of the dramatic changes that take place as the sun rises. Suppose you were lost during the hours of the night. As you see the night decline and the sun begin to rise, you develop a sense of confidence. The darkness is gone. You can see the path before you. The clouds that were so foreboding during the lonely night are now touched by the light of the sun and they become transformed, glowing with metallic brilliance.

Think of wisdom or the vision of God as the rising sun. The moment you catch a glimpse of that dawning of knowledge, the darkness of confusion and misery is gone. The black clouds of troubles turn into blessings. The path before you becomes clear.

Imagine the thrill of nature as the rays of the rising sun touch the clouds, as they shimmer on the rivers and lakes, as they spread across the valleys and the snowy mountain peaks, making those peaks dazzle as if they were covered with gold.

Similarly, imagine the light of the Self, the light of intuition, touching your intellect, sweeping over your mind, spreading out and enveloping your personality.

While repeating the *Gayatri Mantra*, you may chose the *saguna* aspect (the Deity with form) for meditation. You may meditate upon the form of Goddess Gayatri— the Goddess who presides over the *mantra*. Goddess Gayatri is seated on a lotus with ten arms and five faces, and she holds in her hands a conch, a mace, a noose, a bowl, a lotus and other objects.

The many faces and arms are suggestive of the fact that the Goddess (the Divine Self) is all-pervasive. The various objects in her hands are symbols of numerous Divine attributes. The Grace of the Goddess destroys obstacles (this is represented by a mace). There is un-foldment of spirituality in a devotee (this is represented by the lotus). Similarly other objects have their mystic meanings.

Feel that your body and mind, your whole personality, are thrilled by the Divine Presence, just as all of nature is thrilled by the luminous sun at dawn.

Holding this vision of the luminous sun within your mind, and considering the sun as the visible manifestation of the Divine Self, offer adoration to God who permeates the three worlds or the three planes, who is the Light of lights. And having developed that awareness of His presence, dedicate your intellect at the feet of the Divine Self. May He touch your intellect with his enlightening grace.

As your mind enters into the depths of meditation, you will stop the mental repetition of *mantra*. However, the meaning and the feeling of the *mantra* will continue and the symbolic forms may continue to float before your mental vision.

But as you ascend higher, enveloped by the joy of Divine Presence, you will lose awareness of the body, awareness of names and forms, awareness of time and space. When you encounter something so sweet and loving, your mind stops. It transcends time and space.

In that experience of Divine Presence, ego melts. You begin to view all the things that seem real in your life like a passing dream. The real You—the real spirit within you—is not the body. It is not confined to time and space. It is not subject to pleasure and pain. It is transcendental—like the shining sun. It is one with God, the Divine Self—eternal, infinite, the embodiment of bliss.

MEDITATION ON MAHAMRITYUNJAYA MANTRA

ॐ त्र्यम्बकम् यजामहे सुगन्धिम् पुष्टिवर्द्धनम् ।
उर्वारुकमिव बन्धनान् मृत्योर्मुक्षीय माऽमृतात् ॥

Om tryambakam yajaamahe
Sugandhim pushti vardhanam
Urvaarukamiva bandhanaan
Mrityor muksheeya maa amritaat

We adore the Supreme, who is the possessor
of the three eyes (and the three energies),
who is the enhancer of fragrance and nourishment. May we be liberated from the meshes
of death, as a fruit is liberated from the
bondage of creeping vines, and may we be led
to immortality.

This *Vedic* hymn expresses the innermost urge for
immortality which abides in the hearts of all human
beings. Life is a continuous struggle to overcome death

and to win immortality. Every action, every experience, and every condition of life are phases of one's evolution leading to the shining sea of immortality, beyond the darkness and delusion of the world-process.

This hymn, adoring Lord Shiva, was revealed to the ancient seers during their long hours of communion with the Self. The lotus of Divine experience bloomed in the clear lakes of their hearts, inspiring them to compose this verse and many other verses abounding in the *Vedas,* and to present them to the world as keys to open the secret treasures of mystic values.

It is called *Mahamrityunjaya Mantra,* meaning a mystic verse which is the great conqueror of death. *"Maha"* means great, *"mrityu"* means death, and *"jaya"* means victory. Any method that prolongs life is a conqueror of death. However, this *mantra* is called great conqueror because when it is repeated with deep understanding and feeling, it confers liberation, which is the complete cessation of birth and death.

Lord Shiva is the Absolute Self presented in a personified form. Like all forms of Divinity revealed by sages, Shiva's form is a highly mystical and poetic representation of the Absolute. His head is generally covered with matted locks. Matted locks represent mysteries of spiritual life. They also denote the chains of Himalayan mountains, which symbolically represent chains of spiritual thought—the sublime thoughts that arise out of profound meditation.

Further, Lord Shiva has the stream of Ganges flowing from His head. That stream represents wisdom. He also holds on His forehead a crescent moon, which is the symbol of mastery over the mind. The mind, in most people, goes on waxing and waning; but in Lord Shiva it remains a crescent shape all the time. It is eternally under control.

The snakes on Siva's body represent cosmic powers, and the ashes from cremation grounds that cover Him symbolize the mighty power of wisdom which consumes all *karmas* and limitations. Lord Shiva is the embodiment of *sanyasa* or renunciation, and at the same time He is the embodiment of auspiciousness and gentleness.

According to the mystic stories of the *Puranas,* Lord Shiva has a third eye, which, although normally closed, is opened when needed to carry out His Divine destruction. According to the *Puranic* story, Lord Shiva was once practising intense austerity and meditation, and was in deep *samadhi.* At that time, Cupid God, with all his army of temptations, came to distract Shiva from that *samadhi.* After they had unsuccessfully exercised all their charm and power, Cupid finally discharged his flowery arrow at Lord Shiva. Lord Shiva then opened his two eyes and looked around. Then he opened his third eye and fire flashed from His forehead, burning up the Cupid God, who was hiding in the shrubs. Since then, according to the story, the Cupid God exists in an invisible form.

Shiva's third eye, as indicated figuratively in the story, is symbolic of intuitive vision, which destroys ignorance, the source of desire and cupidity.

Mahamrityunjaya Mantra is generally described as the remover of obstacles and the prolonger of life. When you meditate on the *mantra's* deeper meaning and adore the Self in the form of Lord Shiva with profound understanding, you will attain no less than the highest goal of life—liberation. Let us then study the *mantra* word by word and reflect upon its deeper meaning:

Om

Om is not an essential part of this *mantra,* but it has been added to enhance its effect. *Om* is the symbol of the Absolute, or God, and it is a mystic formula for invoking that Supreme Self.

Tryambakam

"Tryambakam" means the three-eyed Deity. As discussed above, Lord Shiva is portrayed as having three eyes. Two eyes see the practical reality of the world. The third eye transcends this world, representing intuitive vision that destroys the world-process. So Lord Shiva has three eyes, implying that although He sustains this practical world and looks after all the practical realities of life, through His third eye He transcends all and is ever established in the Absolute Self.

Still another ancient interpretation of the term *"Tryambakam"* is given by the Sanskrit terms *"Tristrah Ambikam Yasya"*—One who possesses three powers *(Kriya Shakti, Ichha Shakti* and *Jnana Shakti*—the energy of action, the energy of will, and the energy of knowledge). These three *Shaktis* or energies are presided by three Goddesses: Durga, Lakshmi and Saraswati.

Durga is represented as a Deity riding on a lion, Lakshmi stands on a lotus flower, and Saraswati rides on a swan. The esoteric meaning is as follows: In the first stages of spiritual evolution, an aspirant has to overcome the gross obstacles that result from his lower nature. Anger, greed, lust, pride, and other evils are gross impurities. The spiritual energy assumes the role of Durga in this stage and destroys those gross impurities.

Then, with the destruction and sublimation of the gross energy, the lotus of the spirit unfolds in the heart of an aspirant. The bees of excellent virtues are attracted to the blooming lotus. Then spiritual energy assumes the role of Lakshmi and grants the objects of desire and prosperity, both materially and spiritually.

The last stage of the spiritual journey is illumined by the grace of Saraswati, clad in a white, shining garment. Saraswati is the advent of knowledge that dispels all darkness from the heart. She rides on a swan, the symbol of discrimination, and she bears a *vina* which denotes the music of harmony and peace.

Thus, *"Tryambakam"* is that One who possesses these three *Shaktis*. He is the Supreme Being—Lord Shiva.

Yajaamahe

"Yajaamahe" means we propitiate, adore or worship that Deity. Propitiation is a process by which an aspirant brings about the union of his soul with the Divine Self. The individual ego, born of ignorance, is dedicated to that Self. It is poured as an oblation into the shining fire of knowledge that burns in the altar of the heart. This is the highest sacrifice. *"Yajaamahe"* indicates surrender, self-effacement, Divine communion, and Divine absorption.

With the sublimation of the ego, the aspirant becomes conscious of the surging ocean of cosmic life. The individual soul is like a bud in the creeping vine of the world-process. This world-process is constituted of the three *Gunas* or modes of nature. *Tamas* is the principle of inertia, *rajas* is the principle of passion and activity, and *sattwa* is the principle of purity or luminosity.

Every individual soul in its journey to the Absolute has to break the obstacles of *tamas* or dark inertia, to sublimate *rajas* or the restless activity of the mind and senses, and to transcend *sattwa* or purity through the intuitional realization of the Absolute.

The bud of the individual soul blossoms when it receives the rays of Divine wisdom and the showers of Divine grace. The emanation of its fragrance comes with the unfoldment of the latent powers of the soul.

Sugandhim

This term means fragrance. Just as the fragrance of the rose, jasmine, queen-of-the-night and other fragrant flowers delights the heart, so too, with the unfoldment of the spirit, the lotus of the heart blooms and a celestial fragrance emanates in the form of cheerfulness, serenity, purity, cosmic love, compassion, satisfaction, and other Divine qualities.

These virtuous qualities are due to the presence of *shubha samskaras*—spiritual impressions based upon goodness, impressions born of *samadhi* that give rise to experiences of lofty feelings and thoughts, of selflessness, of nonviolence. If you develop such impressions your personality wears a Divine fragrance. That is the spiritual aroma that great men leave behind after they die—the fragrance of the soul.

It is due to lack of fragrance of the soul that a man suffers from various diseases of the body and mind. The source of all diseases is ignorance or *avidya*. It gives rise to diseases of the mind called *adhis*. Mental diseases manifest in the form of anger, greed, hatred, and other impurities that bring about disharmony in the flow and circulation of the vital energy in the body. This causes various diseases of the body known as *vyadhis*. Therefore, by meditating upon the Divine Self, Lord Shiva, as the bestower or enhancer of fragrance, an aspirant removes diseases from his body and his mind.

Pushti Vardhanam

These terms mean the increaser of nourishment. *"Pushti"* means nourishment and *"vardhanam"* means increaser. The Divine Self is He who increases fragrance (*sugandhim*), and nourishment (*pushti*). Nourishment refers to integration of personality. Your personality has four great factors: reason, emotion, will and action. When you receive Lord Shiva's grace, these four become well-balanced and *pushti* or mystic nourishment is enhanced.

Just as a fruit ripens day by day, even so an individual soul acquires maturity in the creeping vine of the world-process and becomes integrated. When a fruit develops, nature enhances ripeness and fragrance in the fruit. Similarly as you grow and mature you are like a fruit and Lord Shiva causes that fruit to ripen. A saint is a ripened fruit in the tree of the world-process.

The Divine Self is the possessor and controller of *prakriti* or nature or *maya* (the power of illusion). He is the source of all nourishment, whether it is of the body, the mind, or the soul. Even if you are in the most adverse conditions, even if you are suffering from the worst malady, turn your mind to God who abides in your heart. Feel that He is infusing you with strength, that He is vibrating in every cell of your body, that His joy is coursing through your veins. You will be relieved of all troubles.

Urvarukamiva

This term refers to a vine-like plant that bears fruit, like the cucumber or pumpkin. As the fruit grows, it is sustained by the plant; but when it is mellowed with sweetness, when it becomes truly ripe, it drops off spontaneously and detaches completely from the mother plant—and cannot be brought back into it again.

Similarly, every individual is like the growing cucumber in the creeper of the world-process. The world-process is described as a creeper because it has many branches or tendrils and it catches hold of everyone through *karmic* entanglements. By Lord Shiva's grace you mature through personality integration, develop Divine virtues, and, the moment ripeness comes, you detach from the world-process, never to return to it again. That freedom from the bondage of ignorance is the great climax of spiritual movement—Self-realization.

Bandhanan Mrityormuksheeya

These words mean liberate us from the bondage of death. Death is the symbol of darkness that hampers the unfoldment of the spirit. *Avidya* or ignorance is the source of death. Egoism, attachment, selfishness, etc., are the meshes of death. The entire world-process is a widespread snair of death. Life is a ceaseless battle against death. Spiritual life leads to the victory over death or the attainment of immortality.

Maa Amritat

These words imply, "Lead me to immortality. May I not be separated from the immortal abode of the Self—*Brahman*." A common fruit falls down and perishes, but not the fruit of the soul that grows on the creeper of the world-process. Having been liberated, it falls into the shining ocean of bliss. It enters into the Supreme Self even as a river enters into the ocean. The soul acquires perfection by transcending the mind, the intellect, the senses. It is established in its essential nature of *Sat Chit Ananda*—Existence, Knowledge, and Bliss Absolute.

Thus, the short but powerful *Mahamrityunjaya Mantra* is a most exquisite flower in the garden of the *Vedas*. It bestows upon its devotees the enjoyments of the world as well as liberation. It fulfills human desires and aspirations, awakens love for the Supreme, decks the soul with excellent virtues, and liberates it from the wheel of birth and death.

May you repeat this *mantra* regularly with insight, feeling and devotion, and may its Divine potency unfold in your heart and lead you to immortality.

Om Namah Shivaaya! (Adorations to Lord Shiva!) May you receive the blessings of Lord Shiva!

About Swami Jyotirmayananda
And His Ashram

Swami Jyotirmayananda was born on February 3, 1931, in a pious family in Dumari Buzurg, District Saran, Bihar, India—a northern province sanctified by the great Lord Buddha. From his early childhood he showed various marks of future saintliness. He was calm and reflective, compassionate to all, and a constant source of inspiration to all who came in contact with him. Side by side with his studies and practical duties, he reflected upon life's deeper purpose.

An overwhelming feeling to serve humanity through a spiritual life led him to embrace the ancient order of Sanyasa on February 3, 1953, at the age of 22. Living in the Himalayan retreats by the sacred River Ganges, he practised intense austerities. In tireless service of his Guru, Sri Swami Sivananda Maharaj, Swamiji taught at the Yoga Vedanta Forest Academy as a professor of religion. In addition to giving lectures on the Upanishads, Raja Yoga and all the important scriptures of India, he was the editor of the Yoga Vedanta Journal. Ever able to assist foreign students in understanding Yoga and Vedanta, his intuitive perception of their problems endeared him to all.

Swamiji's exemplary life, love towards all beings, great command of spiritual knowledge, and dynamic expositions on Yoga and Vedanta philosophy attracted enormous interest all over India. He frequently lectured by invitation at the All India Vedanta Conferences in Delhi, Amritsar, Ludhiana, and in other parts of India.

In 1962, after many requests, Swami Jyotirmayananda came to the West to spread the knowledge of India. As founder of Sanatan Dharma Mandir in Puerto Rico (1962-1969), Swamiji rendered unique service to humanity through his regular classes, weekly radio lectures in English and in Spanish, and numerous TV appearances.

In March, 1969, Swamiji moved to Miami, Florida, and established the Ashram that has become the center for the international activities of the Yoga Research Foundation. Branches of this organization now exist throughout the world, and spread the teachings of Yoga to aspirants everywhere. In 1985, the Indian Ashram near New Delhi opened its doors and is now serving the community by offering Yoga classes, by publishing the Hindi Journal, Yoganjali, and by assisting the needy through a medical clinic.

Today Swami Jyotirmayananda occupies a place of the highest order among the international men of wisdom. He is well-recognized as the foremost proponent of Integral Yoga, a way of life and thought that synthesizes the various aspects of the ancient Yoga tradition into a comprehensive plan of personality integration.

Through insightful lectures that bring inspiration to thousands who attend the conferences, camps and philosophical gatherings, Swamiji shares the range and richness of his knowledge of the great scriptures of the world.

His monthly magazine—International Yoga Guide—is enjoyed by spiritual seekers throughout the world. His numerous books and cassette tapes are enriching the lives of countless aspirants who have longed for spiritual guidance that makes the most profound secrets of Yoga available to them in a manner that is joyous and practical.

Despite the international scope of his activities, Swamiji still maintains an intimate setting at his main Ashram in Miami that allows fortunate aspirants to have the privilege of actually studying and working under his direct guidance. In the lecture hall of the Foundation, Swami Jyotirmayananda personally conducts an intense weekly schedule of classes in Bhagavad Gita, Yoga Vasistha, Mahabharata, Raja Yoga, Upanishads, Panchadashi, the Bible, Hatha Yoga and meditation.

With a Work/Study Scholarship, qualified students are able to attend all classes conducted by Swamiji tuition-free. In return, students devote their energy and talents to the Foundation's noble mission by serving in the bookshop, offices, press, and computer and publication facilities.

Both the Yoga Research Foundation and the main Ashram lie in the southwest section of Miami, two minutes from the University of Miami and 15 minutes from the Miami International Airport. The main Ashram is on a two and a half acre plot surrounded by trees and exotic plants, reminiscent of the forest hermitages of the ancient Sages. Adjoining are subsidiary Ashrams that house student residents and Foundation guests. The grounds are picturesque, abounding with tall eucalyptus and oak trees, a fragrant mango orchard giving shelter to numerous birds and squirrels, and a lake of lotus blooms reflecting the expansion of the sky. In this serene yet dynamic environment, the holy presence of Swami Jyotirmayananda fills the atmosphere with the silent, powerful message of Truth, and the soul is nurtured and nourished, allowing for a total education and evolution of one's Inner Self.

Magazine

Enjoy 12 full months of Yoga's finest with the INTERNATIONAL YOGA GUIDE

Enter your subscription to the International Yoga Guide and get a year's worth of instruction and guidance—a year's worth of intriguing, thought-provoking reading. Month by month come fresh articles, new ideas, and the innovative style that has made Swami Jyotirmayananda's Integral Yoga renowned the world over.

Subscribe now! Along with insightful essays about applying Integral Yoga in your daily life, you'll find articles on:

- Meditation
- Classic Literature
- Questions and Answers
- Exercise
- Spiritual Instructions

Order No. 3
$15/yr
$27/2 yrs
$38/3 yrs
$12/yr for more than 3 yrs
$300.00/lifetime subscription

DUES-FREE MEMBERSHIP

When you subscribe to the International Yoga Guide, you are automatically a member of the Yoga Research Foundation.

All standing member/subscribers are entitled to the following privileges and benefits:

- 10% discount on all cassettes and book orders
- 50% off all IYG back issues
- Personal correspondence with Swami Jyotirmayananda on any question or difficulty

YOGA CAN CHANGE YOUR LIFE
Over 40 articles of practical guidance in applying Integral Yoga to your daily life.
        paper: 240 pgs.   (Order No. 1) $4.99

CONCENTRATION AND MEDITATION
From beginning to advanced—a complete course in itself.
        cloth: 200 pgs.   (2) $9.50

INTERNATIONAL YOGA GUIDE
12 monthly issues of the finest in Yoga teachings.
        (3a) $15.00/yr., (3b) $27.00/2 yr.

YOGA GUIDE
Direct helpful answers to your questions on Yoga and life.
        paper: 270 pgs.   (4) $2.99

THE MYSTERY OF THE SOUL (Katha Upanishad)
In story form, Katha Upanishad reveals its most profound teachings.
        paper: 120 pgs.   (5) $2.99

THE WAY TO LIBERATION, Vols I & II
Yoga philosophy delightfully brought out through stories and dialogue from "Shanti Parva" of the Mahabharata—the well-known epic of India.
        paper: 250 pgs.   (6a, 6b)   each $4.99

YOGA EXERCISES for Health and Happiness
Discover the key to a lifetime of health, beauty and profound peace of mind. More than 200 illustrations.
        paper: 272 pgs.   (7) $4.99

DEATH AND REINCARNATION
Clarifies the mysteries of after-life, reincarnation and the Law of Karma.
        cloth: 198 pgs.   (8) $9.50

RAJA YOGA—STUDY OF MIND
Detailed study allows the reader to experience and control the phenomenon of the mind.
        cloth: 108 pgs.   (9) $9.50

MANTRA, KIRTANA, YANTRA AND TANTRA
Theory and practice of the simplest, most direct method to elevate the mind.
        paper: 64 pgs.   (10) $3.99

HINDU GODS AND GODDESSES
Philosophy and mystic symbolism behind Hindu deities.
        paper: 64 pgs.   (11) $3.99

BEAUTY AND HEALTH through Yoga Relaxation
Tap the boundless resources of the mind through the art of Yoga relaxation.
        paper: 64 pgs.   (12) $1.99

YOGA QUOTATIONS
From the wisdom of Swami Jyotirmayananda, quotes for deep meditation and reflection.
        paper: 240 pgs.   (13) $3.99

Books

YOGA MYSTIC POEMS
Lofty verses reflecting the nature of the inner spirit.
    paper: 240 pgs.   (14) $2.99

YOGA MYSTIC SONGS for Meditation, Vols. I-VII
Spiritual music by Swami Lalitananda promoting a peaceful setting for meditation.
           (15a-g)   each $2.99

YOGA IN LIFE
Practical essays by Swami Lalitananda for quick advancement in Yoga.
    paper: 268 pgs.   (16) $2.99

YOGA MYSTIC STORIES
    paper: 208 pgs.   (17) $3.99

YOGA STORIES AND PARABLES
Charming tales of great philosophical and mystic significance.
    paper: 208 pgs.   (18) $3.99

RAJA YOGA SUTRAS
The original Sutras of Patanjali Maharshi with translation and in-depth commentary.
    paper: 240 pgs.   (19) $2.99

YOGA WISDOM OF THE UPANISHAD
Classical exposition containing the essence of all Yoga philosophy.
    paper: 240 pgs.   (20) $4.99

YOGA SECRETS OF PSYCHIC POWERS
Explore the mysterious powers of the mind in this fascinating manual.
    paper: 208 pgs.   (21) $4.99

JNANA YOGA (Yoga Secrets of Wisdom)
Concise and comprehensive description of the Yoga of Knowledge.
    paper: 64 pgs.   (22) $1.99

VEDANTA IN BRIEF
Acquire a knowledge of the basic structure of Vedanta philosophy in a very short time.
    paper: 244 pgs.   (23) $3.99

YOGA VASISTHA, Vols. I, II & III
Rare account of Sage Vasistha's highest teachings to Lord Rama; the only exposition to be found in the West.
    paper: 288 pgs. ea.   (24a, b, c)   each $4.99

SEX-SUBLIMATION, TRUTH & NON-VIOLENCE
Yoga explanation of basic ethical qualities universally adopted by all religions.
    paper: 208 pgs.   (25) $3.99

APPLIED YOGA
Advanced application of Integral Yoga in your life.
    cloth: 212 pgs.   (26) $9.50

Books

YOGA OF PERFECTION (Srimad Bhagavad Gita)
The most loved and revered scripture in philosophical literature.
paper: 120 pgs.   (27) $3.99

WAKING, DREAM AND DEEP SLEEP
Unravels the puzzling nature of these three states of consciousness.
paper: 64 pgs.   (28) $2.99

INTEGRAL YOGA—A Primer Course
Contains everything you need to get started on the road to a better life.
paper: 112 pgs.   (29) $2.85

YOGA INTEGRAL—Curso Básico
Spanish translation of Integral Yoga—A Primer Course.
Paper: 112 pgs.   (29S) $2.85

YOGA ESSAYS for Self-Improvement
Simple, practical and dynamic ways to life's enhancement.
paper: 248 pgs.   (30) $4.99

THE YOGA OF DIVINE LOVE
A commentary on the Narada Bhakti Sutras.
paper: 240 pgs.   (31) $4.99

INTEGRAL YOGA TODAY
Sunday afternoon talks at Miami's Theosophical Society.
paper: 96 pgs.   (32) $2.50

YOGA OF ENLIGHTENMENT
Chapter 18 of the Bhagavad Gita—Sanskrit, translation and detailed commentary.
paper: 176 pgs.   (33) $5.00

SRIMAD BHAGAVAD GITA
Pocket version with Sanskrit transliteration and English translation by Swami Jyotirmayananda.
paper: 379 pgs.   (34) $4.00

THE ART OF POSITIVE THINKING
Series of articles revealing the power of mind and the techniques used to unlock and cultivate this power.
paper: 145 pgs.   (35) $3.50

EL ARTE DE PENSAR POSITIVAMENTE
Spanish version of The Art of Positive Thinking.
paper: 160 pgs   (35S) $3.50

THE MYSTICISM OF MOTHER WORSHIP
An inspiring and comprehensive exploration of the mysticism behind Devi Puja or Mother Worship.
paper: 70 pgs.   (36) $10.00

ADVICE TO HOUSEHOLDERS
Insight into attaining the highest goal—Self-realization—while achieving harmony within the family unit, and between family and society.
paper: 174 pgs.   (37) $4.95

Cassettes

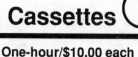

One-hour/$10.00 each

A number after a lecture topic in the following list indicates that there are other cassettes in the list which give insight into the same topic, although the lectures are not related sequentially. If you have difficulty finding any topic you are interested in, please contact us for help.

101
What Happens at the Time of Death
How to Overcome Loneliness #1

102
How to Cooperate with Others #1
How to Educate Your Children #1

103
Karma Yoga #1
How to Develop Vairagya (Dispassion) #1

104
How to Promote Cheerfulness #1
The Teachings of Lord Krishna

105
The Glory of Satsanga #1
How to Remember God #1

106
How to Develop Faith
How to Become a True Disciple #1

107
How to Develop Endurance #1
How to Develop Ahimsa (Non-violence)

108
How to Develop Self-confidence #1
How to Overcome Egoism #1

109
How to Remove Jealousy #1
How to Control Imagination #1

110
How to Overcome Dullness of Mind
How to Live in the Present

111
How to Develop the Art of Listening #1
How to Develop the Art of Speaking #1

112
How to Remove False Pride #1
The Practice of Yoga in the World

113
How to Remove Mental Abnormalities
How to Remove Mental Depression

114
What is True Religion? #1
What is God?

115
How to Study Scriptures
How to Be Magnanimous

116
How to Practice Kundalini Yoga #1
How to Develop Psychic Powers #1

117
Why a Yogi is a Vegetarian
Health in the Light of Yoga #1

118
How to Develop Your Talents
How to Utilize Your Time

119
How to Serve Humanity #1
How to Pray #1

120
How to Develop Discrimination (Viveka) #1
How to Practice Austerity

121
How to Think Positively
How to Promote Wisdom

122
How to be Truly Prosperous
How to Develop the Spirit of Service #2

123
How to Remove Ignorance
How to Develop Spiritual Aspiration

124
Spiritualism vs. Spirituality
How to Practice Meditation

125
How to Practice Truthfulness #1
What is Your Essential Nature

126
How to Withdraw the Senses
How to Educate the Subconscious

127
How to Develop Positive Imagination #2
How to Overcome Procrastination

128
How to Develop Inspiration
How to Overcome Maya

129
How to Cooperate with Others
All Pleasures are Painful to the Wise

130
How to Develop Foresight in Life
Fate and Free Will

131
How to Overcome Hatred #1
How to Enrich Your Life

Cassettes

One-hour/$10.00 each

168
How to Remove Vanity #1
How to Elevate Your Mind #2

169
How to Practice Enquiry of 'Who Am I?' #1
How to Overcome Fear

170
How to Educate Your Children #2
How to Cooperate with Others #3

171
Parapsychology and Yoga
Yoga and Christianity #1

172
How to be Free from the Past #2
How to Practice Japa #2

173
Spiritual Resolves & How to Keep Them #2
How to Remove Anxiety #1

174
How to Develop Intuitional Knowledge
What is the Purpose of Suffering in Life?

175
How to Develop Psychic Powers #2
How to Practice Kundalini Yoga #2

176
How to Practice Truth #2
You are the Architect of Your Destiny #1

177
How to Pray #2
How to Serve Humanity #3

178
How to Develop Self-Confidence #2
Overcome Tendency to Commit Suicide

179
How to Overcome Craving
Overcome Destiny by Self Effort #2

180
Right Conduct and How to Promote It
How to Develop Endurance #2

181
How to Overcome Pride #2
Kriya Yoga

182
How to Practice Integral Yoga
How to Practice Vairagya (Dispassion) #2

183
The Art of Reflection
How to Develop Endurance #3

184
Yoga and Christianity #2
Judaism in the Light of Yoga

185
How to Overcome Greed
How to Practice Adaptability #2

186
Simple Living and High Thinking #1
How to Promote Thought Power

187
Goal of Life
How to Realize 'Inaction' in Action

188
How to Develop Spirit of Renunciation
How to Remove Mental Conflicts

189
Progress and How to Promote It
You are the Architect of Your Destiny #2

190
How to Develop Surrender to God #2
How to Overcome Laziness

191
How to Overcome Mental Stress
Insight into Yoga Ethics

192
How to Enhance Health and Vitality #2
How to Develop Mental Health #2

193
How to be a True Sadhaka (Spiritual aspirant)
How to Overcome Anxiety #2

194
How to Overcome Vanity #2
How to Develop Equal Vision

195
How to Practice Moderation
Enquiry of 'Who Am I?' #2

196
How to See the Positive in Others
Simple Living and High Thinking #2

197
Karma Yoga #2
Raja Yoga

198
Bhakti Yoga
Jnana Yoga

199
How to Attain Mental Serenity
How to Practice Vairagya (Dispassion) #3

200
How to Attain Cosmic Consciousness
How to Practice Self-discipline

201
The Art of Being Selfless
How to Pray #3

202
How to Experience Bliss
How to Overcome Intolerance

203
Parables in Spiritual Teachings
Characteristics of Spiritual Progress

Cassettes

One-hour/$10.00 each

701
Dispassion
Discrimination
Mental Serenity

702
Control of Senses
Faith
Endurance

703
Mental Tranquility
Renunciation of Selfish Actions
Aspiration For Self-Realization

704
Listening
Reflection
Vedantic Med

705
Non-violence
Truth
Sex-restraint

706
Non-stealing
Non-covetousness
How to Overcome Fear

707
As the New Year Begins
Mental and Physical Purity
Contentment
Austerity

708
Study of Scriptures
Repetition Of Mantra
Surrender to God
Attitude Towards Others I

709
Attitude Towards Others II
Building of Character
Fearlessness
Purity of Nature

710
Steadiness In Wisdom
Charity
Renunciation
Absence of Fault-Finding

711
Compassion
Absence of Greed
Absence of Fickleness
Forbearance

712
Humility
Hypocrisy
Arrogance
Pride

713
Good Association
Serenity
Enquiry
Contentment

714
Concentration
Meditation
Samadhi
Repetition of Mantra

715
Intro to Upasana (Devout Meditation)
Om Upasana
Dahara Upasana
Shandilya Upasana

716
Madhu Vidya Upasana
Madhu Vidya Upasana
Antarayami Upasana
Samvarga Upasana

717
Prana Upasana I
Prana Upasana II
Bhuma Upasana
Soham Upasana

718
Akshara Vidya Upasana
Vibhuti Yoga Upasana
Gayatri Upasana
Maha Mrityunjaya Upasana

719
Kundalini Upasana I
Kundalini Upasana II
Kundalini Upasana III
Kundalini Upasana IV

720
Kundalini Upasana V (Muladhara)
Kundalini Upasana VI (Swadhishthana)
Kundalini Upasana VII (Manipura)
Kundalini Upasana VIII (Anahata)

721
Kundalini Upasana IX (Vishuddhi)
Kundalini Upasana X (Ajna)
Kundalini Upasana XI (Sahasrara)
Saguna Upasana I

722
Saguna Upasana II
Saguna Upasana III
Vichar (Enquiry) I
Vichar (Enquiry) II

723
Vichar (Enquiry) III
Vichar (Enquiry) IV
Vichar (Enquiry) V
How to Brighten Intellect

Cassettes

One-hour/$10.00 each

724
Practice of Austerity
Karma Yoga I
Karma Yoga II
Karma Yoga III

725
Controlling Mind
Surrender to God
Self-discipline
Mystic Art of Prayer I

726
Mystic Art of Prayer II
Mystic Art of Prayer III
Your Essential Nature
Secret of Sadhana

727
Positive Thinking I
Positive Thinking II
Positive Thinking III
Positive Thinking IV

728
Positive Thinking V
Positive Thinking VI
Positive Thinking VII
Positive Thinking VIII

729
Spiritual Value of Conflict
Secret of Yoga
Perseverence
Power of Mind

730
Bhavana I (Spiritual Feeling)
Bhavana II
Bhavana III
Bhavana IV

731
Bhavana V
Bhavana VI
Bhavana VII
Bhavana VIII

732
Evil of Procrastination
Spiritual Value of Life
Spiritual Lessons I
Spiritual Lessons II

733
Overcome Maya I
Overcome Maya II
Overcome Maya III
Overcome Maya IV

734
Overcome Maya V
What is Success?
What is True Education?
Glory of Satsanga (Good Association)

735
Selfless Service I
Selfless Service II
Selfless Service III
Develop Sattwa (Purity)

736
Remembrance of God
Self Effort and Divine Grace I
Self Effort and Divine Grace II
Secrets of Success

737
Experience of Enlightenment
Remove Mental Stress I
Remove Mental Stress II
Practice of Detachment

VIDEO TAPES

S-1	Positive Thinking, Vedanta in Practice, Guru Purnima Message.	$45.00
S-2	Satsanga with Swamiji, Insight into Dharma, Law of Karma.	$45.00
S-3	Birthday Message 1987, Christmas Message, Talk on Austerity.	$45.00
H-1	Hatha Yoga	$35.00

Cassettes

45-hour/$5.00 each

800
Art of Self-Discipline
Secret of Renunciation

801
Secret of Self-Restraint
Insight into Faith

802
Overcome Worry I
Overcome Worry II

803
Overcome Worry III
Overcome Worry IV

804
Acquire Contentment
Spiritual Transformation

805
Reflection on Brahman (the Self)I
Reflection on Brahman II

806
Power of Devotion
Remembrance of God

807
Glory Divine Name I
Glory Divine Name II

808
Illusion of World-Process
Tat Twam Asi—THOU ART THAT

809
Insight into Non-Duality
Path of Nivritti (renunciation)

810
The Secret of Freedom
How to be Unshaken by Adversity

811
Disease of the World-Process
Your Spiritual Identity

812
How to Attain Peace
Mystic Art of God-realization

813
How to Develop Divine Virtues
Insight into Ego

814
Insight into Intuition
Insight into Devotion (Bhakti)

815
Overcoming Insecurity in Life I
Overcoming Insecurity in Life II

816
Secrets of Success
Prevent Mental Abnormalities

817
Five States of Mind I
Five States of Mind II

818
Five States of Mind III
Five States of Mind IV

819
Five States of Mind V
Insight into Sadhana (spiritual discipline)

820
Insight into Kleshas (afflictions)
Insight into Vrittis I (thought-waves)

821
Insight into Vrittis II
Insight into Vrittis III

822
Insight into Austerity I
Insight into Austerity II

823
Swadhyaya (Study of Scriptures)
Surrender to God

824
Health and Physical Diseases
Mental Diseases

825
Overcoming Inertia
Overcoming Doubt

826
Overcoming Obstacles
Dream and Deep Sleep

827
Glory of Divine Name I
Glory of Divine Name II

828
Developing Dispassion
Overcoming Pessimism

829
Yogic Skill in Action
Essentials for Self-Realization

830
Qualities of a Karma Yogi
Equal Vision

831
Insight into Willpower I
Insight into Willpower II

832
Insight into Willpower III
Overcome Stress

833
Thought Culture I
Thought Culture II

834
Insight into Sleep I
Insight into Sleep II

835
Dream I
Dream II

Cassettes

45-minute/$5.00 each

836
Insight into Religion
Law of Karma

837
Vedanta in Practice
Quest for Love

838
Insight into Dharma
Rise and Fall of Ego

839
Who Am I? I
Who Am I? II

840
Who Am I? III
Who Am I? IV

841
Three States of Consciousness I
Three States of Consciousness II

842
Three States of Consciousness III
How to Develop Purity of Intellect

843
Insight into Destruction of Vasanas
Insight into Knowledge of Truth

844
Insight into Bondage and Release
Reason and Intuition

845
Quest for Happiness I
Quest for Happiness II

846
Quest for Happiness III
Quest for Happiness IV

847
Philosophy of Action I
Philosophy of Action II

848
Practice of Meditation I
Practice of Meditation II

849
Practice of Meditation III
Art of Relaxing the Mind

850
Insight into Freedom
Insight into Upasana (Devout Meditation)

851
Insight into Spiritual Progress
Insight into Self-effort

852
Insight into Knowledge
Insight into Non-duality

853
Insight into Energy
Prophecy vs. Spirituality

854
Insight into Happiness
How to Overcome Mental Stress

855
How to Develop Cheerfulness
The Virtue of Self-reliance

856
What Is Religion?
Insight into Hinduism

857
The Story of Prahlad
The Story of Druva

858
Message of Divali
The Destruction of Kamsa

859
What is True Education
The Mysticism of Devi Puja

860
Insight into Devotion
Instructions for Developing Devotion

861
Insight into Education
Success in Sadhana

862
Insight into Spiritual Aspiration
Removing Body Idea

863
How to Develop Devotion to God
Your Spiritual Identity

864
Insight into Sadhana
Philosophy of Beauty

865
Insight into Peace
Potentially of the Soul

866
Power of Devotion (Story of Sage Amoarish)
Insight into Non-violence

867
Art of Handling Adversity
Be Practical

868
Divine Incarnation
Presence of God

869
Insight into Spirituality
Yoga in Practice

870
Insight into Grace
The Problem of Sin

871
Overcoming Intolerance
The Spiritual Path

BOOKS: See book list on pages 178—180 for the order number and current price of each book.

CASSETTES: See cassette list on pages 181—188. Cassettes in the 100-700 series are 60 minutes long—$10 each. Cassettes in the 800 series are 45 minutes long—$5 each. Write us also about cassette series on various scriptures such as: *Gita, Upanishads, Bible, Ramayana, Yoga Vasistha, Mahabharata*, etc.

MAGAZINE: INTERNATIONAL YOGA GUIDE—$15/12 monthly issues; $27/2 years; $38/3 yrs; $12/year for more than 3 years; $300/lifetime subscription. Domestic postage prepaid. Foreign postage $6.00 extra/year.

This sheet may be torn out of the book and used as an order form, or it may be photocopied. Or you may simply send us the information in a letter. Be sure, however, to include all information asked for, especially the information on any credit cards used.

ORDER FORM

Telephone Orders: Call (305) 666-2006. Have your VISA or MasterCard ready.

Postal Orders: Please fill out the following information and send to the Yoga Research Foundation, 6111 S.W. 74th Avenue, South Miami, Florida 33143, U.S.A.

Please send the following books or cassettes. I understand that I may return any item for a full refund, or cancel my subscription to the *International Yoga Guide* **magazine for a prorated refund.**

QTY	ORDER NO. / TITLE	EACH	PRICE

MEMBERSHIP: When you subscribe to the *International Yoga Guide*, you are automatically a member of the Yoga Research Foundation. All standing member/subscribers are entitled to 1) A 10% discount on all cassette and book orders, 2) 50% off all IYG back issues, and 3) Personal correspondence with Swami Jyotirmayananda on any question or difficulty.	
SUBTOTAL	
DISCOUNT*	
SUBTOTAL	
POSTAGE	
TOTAL	

Sales Tax: For orders being sent to Florida, please add 6% to your order.

Shipping: 1st item $1.00 (U.S.) or $1.50 (foreign). Add each additional item: $.25 (U.S.) or $.50 (foreign). For magazine postage, see other side.

Name: _____

Address: _____

City: _____ State:_____ Zip:_____

Payment: Please send payment with your order. U.S. customers pay by money order or check payable to the Yoga Research Foundation, or credit card (VISA or MasterCard). Foreign customers pay in U.S. dollars by an international money order or check drawn on a U.S. bank. Please, no cash. All prices subject to change.

Credit Card Orders: VISA or MasterCard:

Card Number: _____ Expiration Date:____/____

Name on Card: _____

Signature: _____

10/89

BOOKS: See book list on pages 178—180 for the order number and current price of each book.

CASSETTES: See cassette list on pages 181—188. Cassettes in the 100-700 series are 60 minutes long—$10 each. Cassettes in the 800 series are 45 minutes long—$5 each. Write us also about cassette series on various scriptures such as: *Gita, Upanishads, Bible, Ramayana, Yoga Vasistha, Mahabharata*, etc.

MAGAZINE: INTERNATIONAL YOGA GUIDE—$15/12 monthly issues; $27/2 years; $38/3 yrs; $12/year for more than 3 years; $300/lifetime subscription. Domestic postage prepaid. Foreign postage $6.00 extra/year.

This sheet may be torn out of the book and used as an order form, or it may be photocopied. Or you may simply send us the information in a letter. Be sure, however, to include all information asked for, especially the information on any credit cards used.

ORDER FORM

Telephone Orders: Call (305) 666-2006. Have your VISA or MasterCard ready.

Postal Orders: Please fill out the following information and send to the Yoga Research Foundation, 6111 S.W. 74th Avenue, South Miami, Florida 33143, U.S.A.

Please send the following books or cassettes. I understand that I may return any item for a full refund, or cancel my subscription to the *International Yoga Guide* magazine for a prorated refund.

QTY	ORDER NO. / TITLE	EACH	PRICE

*MEMBERSHIP: When you subscribe to the *International Yoga Guide*, you are automatically a member of the Yoga Research Foundation. All standing member/ subscribers are entitled to 1) A 10% discount on all cassette and book orders, 2) 50% off all IYG back issues, and 3) Personal correspondence with Swami Jyotirmayananda on any question or difficulty.	SUBTOTAL
	DISCOUNT*
	SUBTOTAL
	POSTAGE
	TOTAL

Sales Tax: For orders being sent to Florida, please add 6% to your order.

Shipping: 1st item $1.00 (U.S.) or $1.50 (foreign). Add each additional item: $.25 (U.S.) or $.50 (foreign). For magazine postage, see other side.

Name: _____

Address: _____

City: _____ State:_____ Zip:_____

Payment: Please send payment with your order. U.S. customers pay by money order or check payable to the Yoga Research Foundation, or credit card (VISA or MasterCard). Foreign customers pay in U.S. dollars by an international money order or check drawn on a U.S. bank. Please, no cash. All prices subject to change.

Credit Card Orders: VISA or MasterCard:

Card Number:_____ Expiration Date:____ / ____

Name on Card: _____

Signature: _____

10/89